IN PURSUIT OF ME!

A 12 Week Pursuit Journal For Women
On The Journey Of Personal Growth & Self Discovery

STEPHANIE M. KIRKLAND

IN PURSUIT OF ME!

You've probably read a million self-help books but how do you apply those ideas into your life and make real and lasting changes?

The weekly and quarterly check-ins keep you committed, accountable & motivated. With a quarterly review that celebrates your achievements and highlights new opportunities for the coming month, each stage lays the foundation for personal growth, reaching your goals and finding and following your purpose.

This beautifully designed journal will inspire you to upgrade your life and achieve your goals. You don't have to wait to start achieving your goals, when you can start today. This journal is used every day and could transform, shape and dynamically alter your life!

Features:

- Weekly Soul Clarity Reflections
- 84 Day Guided Mindset Journal
- Weekly, Quarterly Self Reflection Guide
- Weekly Personal Accountability Sheet
- Weekly Self Care Sheet
- Weekly Comprehensive Affirmation, Vision and Truth Planner
- Life Application Truths, Quotes, and Wisdom
- Monthly Vision Plan
- Prompts and Reminders for Staying on Track
- Un-dated, so you can start anytime

IN PURSUIT OF ME!

The *In Pursuit of ME! 12-Week Pursuit Journal* includes 84 days worth of powerful, actionable wisdom, exercises, truths and focus to help you discover and pursue your personal growth. It's insightful, practical, and creative—a great tool for transformation and growth! The purpose of this journal is to help you transform yourself and your life so that you are focused for 12 weeks on your personal growth. You will be well on the way to DISCOVER, BECOME and EMPOWER your life. You will gain clarity on who you are and what is holding you back. You will also streamline and bring harmony to your life so that you have the space and energy to pursue your purpose.

Every week for twelve weeks, you will take small and manageable steps. Each step reveals aspects of yourself and tools to empower your growth. Each week begins and ends with opportunities to reflect, plan and create specific actions that keep you moving forward week after week.

Through the journal, we covers four main areas:

- Understanding more about yourself;

- Addressing roadblocks and limitations that hold you back;

- Creating a vision for your growth;

- Taking actions that empower your personal growth journey.

You will benefit from the clarity this self-work provides, and you may find the information you uncover about yourself leads you to something unexpected and exciting. As you do the daily Soul Clarity Reflections, you may feel uncomfortable or even sad. Don't shut down, be honest with yourself and about life. The reflections provide information that can reveal who you are and who you need to BECOME to move forward. We need to deal with these internal limitations before we can DISCOVER, BECOME and EMPOWER our lives which creates effective IMPACT on the different roles and responsibilities we walk out on a daily basis as women.

Take your time and stay on track with the schedule. You may be tempted to read ahead, trying to cram 84 days of learning and actions into less time. Believe me, I understand that. But I encourage you to "marinate" and allow the information presented to resonate in your mind, heart, soul and spirit for greater clarity and application

The next84 Days you need to focus and be intentional. Each of the daily, weekly and monthly actions requires time, introspection and reflection. Give yourself the gift of this time and fully complete the process.

When everything "else" is more important than your WELLBEING your priorities are off. Why? Because your WELLBEING determines how you handle and make decisions ABOUT everything "else".
Stephanie M. Kirkland

PERSONAL COMMITTMENT

I, _____, am committed to creating meaningful and lasting change in my life and doing all of the work it requires. As part of this process I will:

1. I will write down in clear language who I want to be. I will provide details and add thoughts to these items daily.

2. I will commit to surround myself with the "right" people and limit exposure to people, things and ideas that are a risk to my success.

3. I will give myself a lot of grace

4. I will make sure I read my goals, journal and talk with supportive people every day to ensure I am making decisions and thinking thoughts that will keep me moving towards my goal.

5. I will keep moving forward EVERY SINGLE DAY.

_____

Signature

_____

Accountability Witness

MY WHY STATEMENT

Your why statement puts in perspective why you are pursuing these next 12 weeks. Remember, your why has to be greater than your excuses in order to succeed.

MONTH

SUNDAY	MONDAY	TUESDAY	WEDNESDAY	THURSDAY	FRIDAY	SATURDAY

NOTES

_____

_____

_____

_____

_____

_____

_____

MONTHLY GOAL PLAN

What is your vision for this month. When we write our vision it helps us bring focus. When you have focus you can get clarity about the steps necessary to move

1

	1
	2
	3

1	2	3	4	5	6	7	8	9	10	11	12	13	14	15
16	17	18	19	20	21	22	23	24	25	26	27	27	29	30

Goal   Action Steps

2

	1
	2
	3

1	2	3	4	5	6	7	8	9	10	11	12	13	14	15
16	17	18	19	20	21	22	23	24	25	26	27	27	29	30

Goal   Action Steps

3

	1
	2
	3

1	2	3	4	5	6	7	8	9	10	11	12	13	14	15
16	17	18	19	20	21	22	23	24	25	26	27	27	29	30

WEEK 1

Change is necessary in order to see another outcome in your life. You can't just change your behavior because it won't last. Change begins WITHIN with your beliefs and mindset. ABOUT what you want to change.
Stephanie M. Kirkland

WHERE AM I NOW?

First, rate from 0 to 10 how much you believe each of the following statements. 0 means you completely disbelieve it. 10 means you think it is completely true.

I have a vision for my life

I have a plan to see my dreams, vision and purpose manifest

I work on my goals daily

I am learning about my dream, vision and purpose

I know who I need to "become" to see my dream manifest

I am disciplined

I spend my time constructively

I am waiting on God to manifest my dream, vision and purpose

I know what I should be doing to see my vision

I'd rather be me than someone else

My mindset is clear about where I am going

PERSONAL REFLECTION

_____
_____
_____
_____
_____
_____
_____
_____
_____

WEEKLY SELF REFLECTION

THIS WEEK I CAN

I NEED TO IMPROVE

MY GOAL THIS WEEK IS

WAYS TO REACH MY GOAL

1.

2.

3.

4.

5.

WEEKLY ACCOUNTABILITY

HEALTHY CHOICES

_____
_____
_____
_____
_____
_____
_____
_____
_____
_____
_____
_____

ACCOUNTABILITY

Wake Time _____
Quiet Time _____
Exercise _____
Power Time _____
Bed Time _____
_____

IMPORTANT THINGS TO DO

_____
_____
_____
_____
_____
_____
_____
_____
_____
_____
_____
_____
_____
_____

CALLS

_____
_____
_____
_____
_____
_____
_____

I AM

TRUTHS

I AM is about declaring NOW who you are irregardless of if it is manifested. We SPEAK to BECOME.

What wisdom, scripture, poem, or declaration are you standing on.

1.

2.

3.

4.

5.

6.

7.

8.

9.

10.

_____

_____

_____

_____

_____

_____

_____

VISION BOARD

Add and Draw picture(s) to keep before your eyes that you want manifested in your life.

WEEKLY SELF CARE PLAN

A Self Care Plan is about things you do for yourself. We are always giving out to others and you need to also give to yourself. How we express in action to others, should come from a place of "love" for yourself. You can't give what you don't have to give.

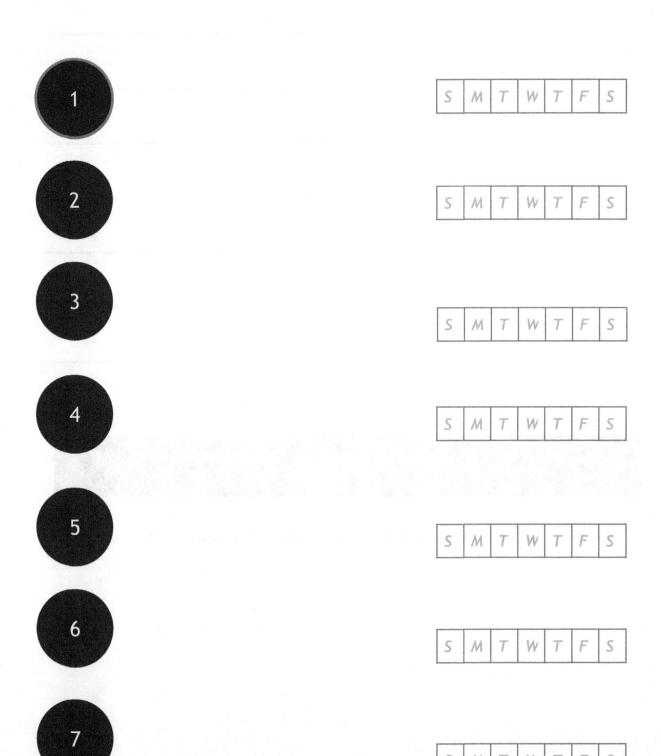

	S	M	T	W	T	F	S
1							
2							
3							
4							
5							
6							
7							

Soul Clarity Reflection

Now

What are you doing NOW. You have to ask yourselves this very important question. It is easy to get caught up in DREAMS, the FUTURE, a VISION; but these things are manifested as a result of our daily activities. A lot of times you live in your DREAMS in order to avoid the work or you are afraid to move forward. It is easier to dream than the daily activity needed for it to manifest.

Your DREAM, FUTURE or VISION, doesn't just suddenly appear because you want it to appear. There are things to learn, develop, create and plan that will cost you something. I heard this statement a couple of weeks ago. It really hit a home run in my heart and is appropriate for this Soul Clarity Reflection. It says, "THE PERSON YOU ARE TODAY, GOT YOU TO THE PLACE YOU ARE TODAY but THE PERSON YOU ARE TODAY, CAN'T GET YOU TO WHERE YOU ARE GOING." This is really a great statement! Who you are right now needs to be developed to move you forward to who you desire to be. Who you are today doesn't have the CAPACITY TO PRODUCE YOUR FUTURE or you would be experiencing the manifestation of your desires Today. Your knowledge level, beliefs, values, fears, perspectives, mentors, passions and discipline all play a part in us reaching the GOAL. Until these areas are DEVELOPED for where you are going, you will not see it manifest because it takes MORE to get to the next place in your development and growth. What are you spending your time on? Who are you spending your time with? How are you spending your time? Each of these questions can be answered NOW!!! Again, it is our NOW that paves the way for where you are going. Yessssss! God is the orchestrator of your life, but according to 2 Peter 1:3, HE HAS GIVEN US ALL THINGS THAT PERTAIN TO LIFE and GODLINESS ALREADY!!! So, you are not

Points to Ponder

1.   NOW you need to decide what you are doing in your daily activity that helps you to obtain your goals.

2.   NOW you need to develop your mindset for where you are going

3.   NOW you need to find the areas of your life you need to grow in, that could be a hinderance.

4.   NOW you need to make up your mind to discipline your life for the prize.

DAY 1

On your journey of Personal Growth and Self Discovery you must learn to maximize everything that makes you who you are. This includes your mind, body, spirit and soul. If you neglect yourself you are not living your life to the fullest. The accumulation of "things" should not be how you define or express who you are. There is nothing wrong with things, but when it "replaces" you taking the time to develop the essence of who you are, it becomes a substitute for authentic living. It becomes a facade that can't replace true identity.

What stands out to me in this Reflection?

_____
_____
_____
_____

What do I need to Change to Live this Fully?

_____
_____
_____
_____

How will I Live this Today?

_____
_____
_____
_____

What does this Reflection mean to Me?

_____
_____
_____
_____
_____
_____
_____
_____

What is your Affirmation to Remind you to Live this Fully Today?

_____
_____
_____

DAY 2

YOU are needed for such a time as this. It doesn't matter how you got here, you are here. Each of us has something to offer our realm of influence. It is selfish to keep it to yourself. It begin with you developing who you are so your journey in turn become a testament that someone can reflect on for their journey. It will be a natural expression because it is your journey. It will be powerful because it is your truth. It will impact because you made it. Someone needs YOU!

What stands out to me in this Reflection?

_____
_____
_____
_____

What do I need to Change to Live this Fully?

_____
_____
_____
_____

How will I Live this Today?

_____
_____
_____
_____

What does this Reflection mean to Me?

_____
_____
_____
_____
_____
_____
_____
_____

What is your Affirmation to Remind you to Live this Fully Today?

_____
_____
_____

DAY 3

You must settle that you are Chosen by God for your INDIVIDUAL and Unique purpose and it is a manifestation of your identity. Your identity is how you express who are as a individual through your behavior that is seen and identified by those around you. Your behavior is made up of your beliefs and supported by your values. We are suppose to LIVE what we believe not just say what we believe because your beliefs shape your behavior. Your beliefs and values should be developed through the truths and principles of your faith. If you don't you will continue searching for direction that God has already given which is to choose LIFE and live.

What stands out to me in this Reflection?

_____
_____
_____
_____

What do I need to Change to Live this Fully?

_____
_____
_____
_____

How will I Live this Today?

_____
_____
_____
_____

What does this Reflection mean to Me?

_____
_____
_____
_____
_____
_____
_____
_____

What is your Affirmation to Remind you to Live this Fully Today?

_____
_____
_____

DAY 4

When you learn to live authentically you will produce light. Authenticity is living your life based on your beliefs and values which shape the very essence of who you are. Your light is not meant to be dimmed. It is meant to shine. When it shines it will irritate those who are comfortable in darkness but let your light so shine!! You don't dim your light to conform to darkness, people are suppose to conform to the light. Your light produces GOOD WORKS that is suppose to be seen and God glorified as a result of it. You are a light everywhere you go today and everyday, so SHINE!

What stands out to me in this Reflection?

_____
_____
_____
_____

What do I need to Change to Live this Fully?

_____
_____
_____
_____

How will I Live this Today?

_____
_____
_____
_____

What does this Reflection mean to Me?

_____
_____
_____
_____
_____
_____
_____
_____
_____

What is your Affirmation to Remind you to Live this Fully Today?

_____
_____
_____

DAY 5

You must not lose yourself by becoming what other people want you to be, instead of being who you really are. Who you look at everyday in the mirror must become someone you know and not someone you have gotten so far away from because the foundation that was suppose to make you whole wasn't there. You must stop living in the past. It is NOW your responsibility to shape your future by being intentional about developing and doing the Self Discovery work by being honest and forthcoming with yourself.

What stands out to me in this Reflection?

_____
_____
_____
_____

What do I need to Change to Live this Fully?

_____
_____
_____
_____

How will I Live this Today?

_____
_____
_____
_____

What does this Reflection mean to Me?

_____
_____
_____
_____
_____
_____
_____
_____

What is your Affirmation to Remind you to Live this Fully Today?

_____
_____
_____

DAY 6

Loving yourself begins with accepting who you are today (good and bad). Don't wait until you become who you would prefer to be. You are the person you have to live with for the rest of your life. So, if you don't learn how to love yourself, you will not be able to love other people effectively. The reasons you have for why you should not love yourself will then be used on those around you. You will become a critical judge instead of an accepting and empowering force in the lives of those you are called to touch. Love begins with you being able to love yourself unconditionally. You are worthy of love and to be accepted for who you are even in your imperfection.

What stands out to me in this Reflection?

_____
_____
_____
_____

What do I need to Change to Live this Fully?

_____
_____
_____
_____

How will I Live this Today?

_____
_____
_____
_____

What does this Reflection mean to Me?

_____
_____
_____
_____
_____
_____
_____
_____

What is your Affirmation to Remind you to Live this Fully Today?

_____
_____
_____

DAY 7

I am what God says I am, not what life has dictated. Your experiences must be viewed as opportunities to learn and grow not a dictate that where you are today is where you must stay. You can bloom through every circumstance with a focus and attitude that you always win. What you are going through will not be able to compare with the wisdom and knowledge you gain as a result of never giving up. The lessons will teach and "mature" you for purpose. You choose to come out better and not bitter.

What stands out to me in this Reflection?

_____

_____

_____

_____

What do I need to Change to Live this Fully?

_____

_____

_____

_____

How will I Live this Today?

_____

_____

_____

_____

What does this Reflection mean to Me?

_____

_____

_____

_____

_____

_____

_____

_____

What is your Affirmation to Remind you to Live this Fully Today?

_____

_____

_____

WEEKLY REVIEW

THIS WEEK:

NEXT WEEK:

2 FAVORITE MEMORIES

2 WAYS I CAN HELP OTHERS

3 PLACES I WANT TO GO

3 THINGS I'M GRATEFUL FOR

1 THING I WANT TO GET BETTER AT

1 HARD LESSON LEARNED

2 THINGS I AM LOOKING FORWARD TO

1 THING I DID THIS WEEK I'M PROUD OF

3 NEW THINGS I WANT TO TRY

WEEK 2

WHERE AM I NOW?

First, rate from 0 to 10 how much you believe each of the following statements. 0 means you completely disbelieve it. 10 means you think it is completely true.

It is hard for me to learn from my negative experiences
I feel that I don't have to change it is the other person
I feel out of control when negative things happen in my life
I am in control of the situations in my life
I can heal from the hurtful situation in my life
I know how to get space from the issue
It doesn't matter if I heal from the situation
I understand all my feelings during this time
I speak over my life daily
I feel I am stuck in a negative cycle

PERSONAL REFLECTION

_____
_____
_____
_____
_____
_____
_____
_____

WEEKLY SELF REFLECTION

THIS WEEK I CAN

I NEED TO IMPROVE

MY GOAL THIS WEEK IS

WAYS TO REACH MY GOAL

1.

2.

3.

4.

5.

WEEKLY ACCOUNTABILITY

HEALTHY CHOICES

_____
_____
_____
_____
_____
_____
_____
_____
_____
_____
_____

ACCOUNTABILITY

Wake Time _____
Quiet Time _____
Exercise _____
Power Time _____
Bed Time _____
_____

IMPORTANT THINGS TO DO

_____
_____
_____
_____
_____
_____
_____
_____
_____
_____
_____
_____
_____

CALLS

_____
_____
_____
_____
_____
_____
_____

I AM

I AM is about declaring NOW who you are irregardless of if it is manifested. We SPEAK to BECOME.

TRUTHS

What wisdom, scripture, poem, or declaration are you standing on.

1.

2.

3.

4.

5.

6.

7.

8.

9.

10.

_____

_____

_____

_____

_____

_____

_____

VISION BOARD

Add and Draw picture(s) to keep before your eyes that you want manifested in your life.

WEEKLY SELF CARE PLAN

A Self Care Plan is about things you do for yourself. We are always giving out to others and you need to also give to yourself. How we express in action to others, should come from a place of "love" for yourself. You can't give what you don't have to give.

S	M	T	W	T	F	S

S	M	T	W	T	F	S

S	M	T	W	T	F	S

S	M	T	W	T	F	S

S	M	T	W	T	F	S

S	M	T	W	T	F	S

S	M	T	W	T	F	S

Even That!

You can learn so much from your negative experiences. That doesn't sound right when you are in the mix but it will in due time. You must CHANGE your perspective and get on the offense. Turn the authority of the situation to YOUR advantage. You can NEVER allow yourself to stay on the defense. When you are on the defense you are not in control. You find yourself waiting to react to what someone or something else is doing. Remember you are in control of the direction of your life! You make the decisions that effect your future. TAKE BACK YOUR AUTHORITY!! You (in concert with God) should be the one who orchestrates what circumstances bring to your life.

Points to Ponder

1. **You need to heal and that is time sensitive.**

Hurt takes time. You will rise and God will be glorified even in this. Allow your truth to soothe the area. Don't continue to return to the circumstance.

2. **You must on purpose refocus on the work you are called to do.**

Focusing on your purpose, your relationship with God, upcoming events in your life keeps you from meditating on things that can push you back into an emotional cycle. Shut down imaginations that lifts itself against your truth! Maybe you and a girlfriend can go out and have some fun?! Your thought life is imperative during this time.

3. **Give yourself space from the issue**.

You are not strong or healed because you can talk about it or deal with whatever you are going through. Empower other areas of your life by spending quality time there

4. **Allow yourself the time to deal with the issue(s) (it's natural).**

Ignoring it's existence doesn't make it go away. To many times we think this is the "spiritual" thing to do. The church is the only place where we "IGNORE" real issues. Say your peace, journal, or speak to someone who is spiritually mature.

5. **Don't try to be the BIG DOG!**

Stop saying it doesn't matter, etc. (it does)The enemy will use your weaknesses, hurts, and issues against you. What happened does matter but don't let it consume your life.

6. **Walk in truth**

You won't feel like it, you may even be numb but that doesn't dictate it's effectiveness. The emotional upheaval will pass. Walk in your truth.

7. **Identify your feelings**.

Start there in your search for truths to hold on to.

8. **Definitely write**.

I am an avid journaler. It helps you to focus and you will see your true feelings and what is in your heart.

9. **You have a future**.

Speak your future desires into existence.

Questions

1.What areas in your life do you need to heal?

2. What are you going to focus on in your life?

3. What alternative thoughts are you going to use when the situation comes up?

DAY 8

You need people in your lives who ACCEPTS you for who you are but expects you to GROW. They PRESS you towards your BEST SELF because they can see the potential and seed of GREATNESS on the inside of you.

What stands out to me in this Reflection?

_____
_____
_____
_____

What do I need to Change to Live this Fully?

_____
_____
_____
_____

How will I Live this Today?

_____
_____
_____
_____

What does this Reflection mean to Me?

_____
_____
_____
_____
_____
_____
_____
_____

What is your Affirmation to Remind you to Live this Fully Today?

_____
_____
_____

DAY 9

Stop trying to SALVAGE things (relationships, circumstances) in your life that need to DIE. It is HOLDING UP future possibilities. It is like a flower dying in the garden. You need toPRUNE so the new flower can have SPACE to grow.

What stands out to me in this Reflection?

_____
_____
_____
_____

What do I need to Change to Live this Fully?

_____
_____
_____
_____

How will I Live this Today?

_____
_____
_____
_____

What does this Reflection mean to Me?

_____
_____
_____
_____
_____
_____
_____
_____

What is your Affirmation to Remind you to Live this Fully Today?

_____
_____
_____

DAY 10

Stay FOCUSED on the goal. Distractions will come so be CAREFUL! They don't always present themselves in a NEGATIVE light, so be mindful of whatever pulls you away from your INTENDED end.

What stands out to me in this Reflection?

_____
_____
_____
_____

What do I need to Change to Live this Fully?

_____
_____
_____
_____

How will I Live this Today?

_____
_____
_____
_____

What does this Reflection mean to Me?

_____
_____
_____
_____
_____
_____
_____
_____

What is your Affirmation to Remind you to Live this Fully Today?

_____
_____
_____

DAY 11

Be WILLING to admit you can be WRONG instead of insisting you are ALWAYS right.
You GAIN respect and growth when you are willing to look at yourself.

What stands out to me in this Reflection?

_____
_____
_____
_____

What do I need to Change to Live this Fully?

_____
_____
_____
_____

How will I Live this Today?

_____
_____
_____
_____

What does this Reflection mean to Me?

_____
_____
_____
_____
_____
_____
_____
_____

What is your Affirmation to Remind you to Live this Fully Today?

_____
_____
_____

DAY 12

GOD took the time to make you uniquely YOU! There is NO ONE like you in the whole world. Your HEIGHT, Your COLOR, Your EYES, Your SMILE, all have a PURPOSE that empowers and impacts.

What stands out to me in this Reflection?

_____
_____
_____
_____

What do I need to Change to Live this Fully?

_____
_____
_____
_____

How will I Live this Today?

_____
_____
_____
_____

What does this Reflection mean to Me?

_____
_____
_____
_____
_____
_____
_____
_____

What is your Affirmation to Remind you to Live this Fully Today?

_____
_____
_____

DAY 13

When you don't walk into your destiny you effect those attached to you. When you aren't where you should be others lack what they are suppose to be getting from you. What is holding you back?

What stands out to me in this Reflection?

_____
_____
_____
_____

What do I need to Change to Live this Fully?

_____
_____
_____
_____

How will I Live this Today?

_____
_____
_____
_____

What does this Reflection mean to Me?

_____
_____
_____
_____
_____
_____
_____
_____

What is your Affirmation to Remind you to Live this Fully Today?

_____
_____
_____

DAY 14

You need to know why people are in your life. They could be holding up someone else's spot. They could be a distraction to keep you off focus or someone to TAKE YOU TO DESTINY.

What stands out to me in this Reflection?

_____
_____
_____
_____

What do I need to Change to Live this Fully?

_____
_____
_____
_____

How will I Live this Today?

_____
_____
_____
_____

What does this Reflection mean to Me?

_____
_____
_____
_____
_____
_____
_____
_____

What is your Affirmation to Remind you to Live this Fully Today?

_____
_____
_____

WEEKLY REVIEW

THIS WEEK:

2 FAVORITE MEMORIES

3 THINGS I'M GRATEFUL FOR

1 HARD LESSON LEARNED

1 THING I DID THIS WEEK I'M PROUD OF

NEXT WEEK:

2 WAYS I CAN HELP OTHERS

3 PLACES I WANT TO GO

1 THING I WANT TO GET BETTER AT

2 THINGS I AM LOOKING FORWARD TO

3 NEW THINGS I WANT TO TRY

WEEK 3

WHERE AM I NOW?

First, rate from 0 to 10 how much you believe each of the following statements. 0 means you completely disbelieve it. 10 means you think it is completely true.

You have mentors and relationships in your life.
Television, Music Artist and Cultural Icons play a big role in who influences me.
The bible is my greatest influence
I can name my values
I spend time reading information that supports my values
I am careful about what I participate in
I am open to listen to people who don't believe what I believe
I am aware of what is going on around me
People see me as a influence
I am a positive influence on others

PERSONAL REFLECTION

_____
_____
_____
_____
_____
_____
_____
_____

WEEKLY SELF REFLECTION

THIS WEEK I CAN

I NEED TO IMPROVE

MY GOAL THIS WEEK IS

WAYS TO REACH MY GOAL

1.

2.

3.

4.

5.

WEEKLY ACCOUNTABILITY

HEALTHY CHOICES

_____
_____
_____
_____
_____
_____
_____
_____

ACCOUNTABILITY

Wake Time _____
Quiet Time _____
Exercise _____
Power Time _____
Bed Time _____
_____

IMPORTANT THINGS TO DO

_____
_____
_____
_____
_____
_____
_____
_____
_____
_____
_____
_____

CALLS

_____
_____
_____
_____
_____
_____

I AM

I AM is about declaring NOW who you are irregardless of if it is manifested. We SPEAK to BECOME.

1.

2.

3.

4.

5.

6.

7.

8.

9.

10.

TRUTHS

What wisdom, scripture, poem, or declaration are you standing on.

_____

_____

_____

_____

_____

_____

_____

VISION BOARD

Add and Draw picture(s) to keep before your eyes that you want manifested in your life.

WEEKLY SELF CARE PLAN

A Self Care Plan is about things you do for yourself. We are always giving out to others and you need to also give to yourself. How we express in action to others, should come from a place of "love" for yourself. You can't give what you don't have to give.

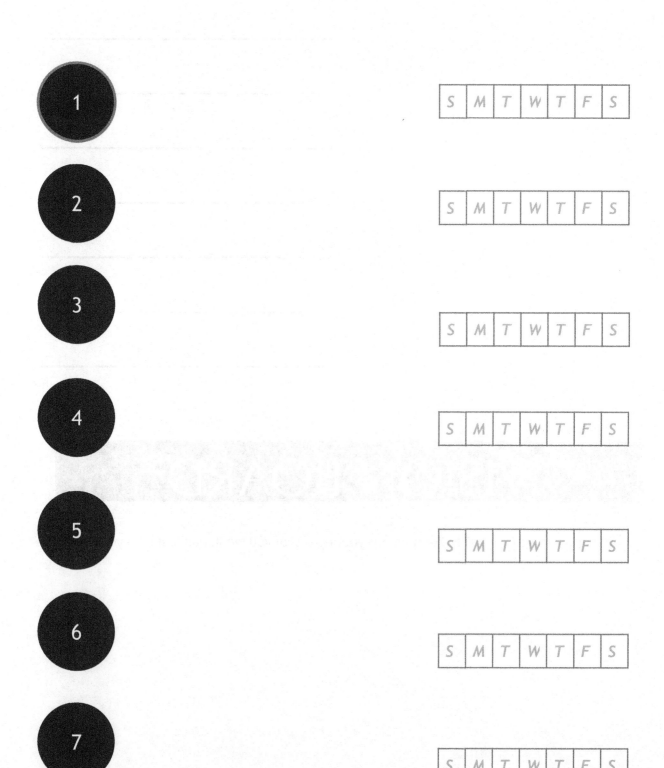

Soul Clarity Reflection

Influence

The great leaders of the Old Testament were always admonishing the people to be mindful of the influences of the world around them. They understood that as they came into contact with other cultures and religions, they had to be settled that their lifestyle practice was their STANDARD. Many did not heed the warnings. You are being charged to pay attention and move forward in a different direction for purpose. There is a need for you to make yourself available and trust God with your destiny and purpose. Through ignorance you can entertain other perspectives that don't support your vision. As a result you can begin to loose what God had planted in your life because you were no longer cultivating the truths of your lifestyle of faith and focus towards purpose. Eventually you can release who you are totally. You must be mindful of what is influencing your life. The more you see, hear and interact with things the more influence they have on your behavior. Even though you may not outwardly practice these things in your life, you no longer see the "harm" in them.

Points to Ponder

1. Analyze your value system.

Your values are the boundary keepers of your decisions. What is and isn't acceptable? Make sure your values are being represented in all your decisions. Sometimes you can react with your flesh and not your values. It is something that you have accepted to handle the circumstance, but it is not within the context of what you hold dear through truth.

2. Use Wisdom

Wisdom is the principle thing. In all thy getting, get understanding. These are powerful words found in scripture. This lets you know that scripture quoting is just the beginning. You must take it to the next. level. The next level is wisdom. Wisdom is "experienced" truth. It is your ability to make scripture relevant to your daily life. God used wisdom to create the universe. Solomon used wisdom to rule his Kingdom. You need to use wisdom to guide your daily life.

3. Analyze what you spend your time doing.

If you will take the time to analyze your life you will see what influences you. What do you read? What do you watch on television? What do you listen to on the radio? Who do you spend time with? Whatever has the majority of your time is your main influence! I know you love the Lord. I know you believe He is God, but what do you allow in your space "THE MOST" ? THAT is what is influencing your decision and life process.

DAY 15

You need to work on becoming your best self because it stops you from devaluing yourself. When you don't understand what you have to contribute, you begin to compare yourself to others because you don't feel adequate. When you begin working on yourself, your focus is not on other people but how you

What stands out to me in this Reflection?

_____
_____
_____
_____

What do I need to Change to Live this Fully?

_____
_____
_____
_____

How will I Live this Today?

_____
_____
_____
_____

What does this Reflection mean to Me?

_____
_____
_____
_____
_____
_____
_____
_____

What is your Affirmation to Remind you to Live this Fully Today?

_____
_____
_____

DAY 16

CHANGE begins with KNOWLEDGE. There is NO WAY around it. Just saying you want "MORE" (money, better job, better relationship, even more of GOD) will not get you to your DESTINATION. There must be a SHIFT in the MIND and the DISCIPLINE to do it.

What stands out to me in this Reflection?

_____
_____
_____
_____

What do I need to Change to Live this Fully?

_____
_____
_____
_____

How will I Live this Today?

_____
_____
_____
_____

What does this Reflection mean to Me?

_____
_____
_____
_____
_____
_____
_____
_____

What is your Affirmation to Remind you to Live this Fully Today?

_____
_____
_____

DAY 17

BE YOUR BEST. Don't just do your best because you don't want people to talk BAD about or confront you. BE YOUR BEST because it is a REFLECTION of YOU. No matter WHAT you do or WHO you do it for it still REPRESENTS you.

What stands out to me in this Reflection?

_____
_____
_____
_____

What do I need to Change to Live this Fully?

_____
_____
_____
_____

How will I Live this Today?

_____
_____
_____
_____

What does this Reflection mean to Me?

_____
_____
_____
_____
_____
_____
_____
_____

What is your Affirmation to Remind you to Live this Fully Today?

_____
_____
_____

DAY 18

Everyday you are going to have to make decisions about how you are going to handle the circumstances of your life. As free will agents, the ability to choose what path to take is a privilege given to us by God. The privilege was sealed in the Garden of Eden. God set the tree in the Garden and told them not to partake of it. He was letting you know that in the midst of the challenges of life, you can overcome whatever temptation that has been brought your way by choosing to do things God's way (even when you don't see the reasoning for it.)

What stands out to me in this Reflection?

_____
_____
_____
_____

What do I need to Change to Live this Fully?

_____
_____
_____
_____

How will I Live this Today?

_____
_____
_____
_____

What does this Reflection mean to Me?

_____
_____
_____
_____
_____
_____
_____
_____

What is your Affirmation to Remind you to Live this Fully Today?

_____
_____
_____

DAY 19

Your VALUE of YOURSELF should carry more weight than the OPINIONS of others. Just say to YOURSELF THEIR LOSS!

What stands out to me in this Reflection?

_____
_____
_____
_____

What do I need to Change to Live this Fully?

_____
_____
_____
_____

How will I Live this Today?

_____
_____
_____
_____

What does this Reflection mean to Me?

_____
_____
_____
_____
_____
_____
_____
_____
_____

What is your Affirmation to Remind you to Live this Fully Today?

_____
_____
_____

DAY 20

DECIDE how you are going to LIVE your life and DO what is NECESSARY to make it a reality. God has GIVEN you His word. You must apply it.

What stands out to me in this Reflection?

_____
_____
_____
_____

What do I need to Change to Live this Fully?

_____
_____
_____
_____

How will I Live this Today?

_____
_____
_____
_____

What does this Reflection mean to Me?

_____
_____
_____
_____
_____
_____
_____
_____

What is your Affirmation to Remind you to Live this Fully Today?

_____
_____
_____

DAY 21

Your ATTITUDE is a REFLECTION of your view of the world and will determine what is AVAILABLE to you. It begins and ends with YOU. Are you sarcastic or positive, suspicious or trusting, pessimistic or optimistic, positive or negative, nasty or easy to get along.

What stands out to me in this Reflection?

_____
_____
_____
_____

What do I need to Change to Live this Fully?

_____
_____
_____
_____

How will I Live this Today?

_____
_____
_____
_____

What does this Reflection mean to Me?

_____
_____
_____
_____
_____
_____
_____
_____
_____

What is your Affirmation to Remind you to Live this Fully Today?

_____
_____
_____

WEEKLY REVIEW

THIS WEEK:

NEXT WEEK:

2 FAVORITE MEMORIES

2 WAYS I CAN HELP OTHERS

3 PLACES I WANT TO GO

3 THINGS I'M GRATEFUL FOR

1 THING I WANT TO GET BETTER AT

1 HARD LESSON LEARNED

2 THINGS I AM LOOKING FORWARD TO

1 THING I DID THIS WEEK I'M PROUD OF

3 NEW THINGS I WANT TO TRY

WEEK 4

WHERE AM I NOW?

First, rate from 0 to 10 how much you believe each of the following statements. 0 means you completely disbelieve it. 10 means you think it is completely true.

My circumstances determine if I am happy

I am easily influenced by others regarding how i feel

I am distracted by the emotions of others

I can name my values

It is easy for me to focus when circumstances are hard

I can be happy no matter what

I resort to my old habits after deciding to act differently

I am aware of what is going on around me

It is God's responsibility to make me happy

I can only be happy when things are good

PERSONAL REFLECTION

_____

_____

_____

_____

_____

_____

_____

_____

WEEKLY SELF REFLECTION

THIS WEEK I CAN

I NEED TO IMPROVE

MY GOAL THIS WEEK IS

WAYS TO REACH MY GOAL

1.

2.

3.

4.

5.

WEEKLY ACCOUNTABILITY

HEALTHY CHOICES

_____
_____
_____
_____
_____
_____
_____
_____
_____
_____
_____
_____

ACCOUNTABILITY

Wake Time   _____
Quiet Time   _____
Exercise   _____
Power Time   _____
Bed Time   _____
             _____

IMPORTANT THINGS TO DO

_____
_____
_____
_____
_____
_____
_____
_____
_____
_____
_____
_____
_____
_____
_____
_____

CALLS

_____
_____
_____
_____
_____
_____
_____
_____

I AM

TRUTHS

I AM is about declaring NOW who you are irregardless of if it is manifested. We SPEAK to BECOME.

What wisdom, scripture, poem, or declaration are you standing on.

1.

2.

3.

4.

5.

6.

7.

8.

9.

10.

_____

_____

_____

_____

_____

_____

_____

VISION BOARD

Add and Draw picture(s) to keep before your eyes that you want manifested in your life.

WEEKLY SELF CARE PLAN

A Self Care Plan is about things you do for yourself. We are always giving out to others and you need to also give to yourself. How we express in action to others, should come from a place of "love" for yourself. You can't give what you don't have to give.

1   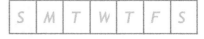

S	M	T	W	T	F	S

2

S	M	T	W	T	F	S

3   

S	M	T	W	T	F	S

4   

S	M	T	W	T	F	S

5   

S	M	T	W	T	F	S

6   

S	M	T	W	T	F	S

7

S	M	T	W	T	F	S

Soul Clarity Reflection

Experiencing Happy

Hannah found herself in an interesting situation. She was a woman who honored God, but she wasn't fulfilled. Hannah was barren and she was in need of a MIRACLE. She felt that her circumstance kept her from fulfilling her purpose and feeling Happy. During that time it was of vital importance and necessity for women to have children. Women were rejected by their husbands, divorced, ridiculed, even called cursed when they could not have children. HANNAH felt rejected, unheard, lost and EVEN cursed by God. Even thou her husband did everything in his power to show her he loved her; she couldn't fill the void. Hannah stopped socializing, became depressed, stopped eating and shut herself off from her husband. She was also being harassed constantly by her husband's other wife PENNIAH.

Just like Hannah, we too can find ourselves loving God and yet in the middle of not feeling fulfilled. How many know what it's like to want something... but don't feel you have what you need to do it. Just like HANNAH you begin to feel separated, unheard, lost and without direction. But Ladies understand that your circumstance doesn't have to keep you from YOUR HAPPY!

So this week, let's EXPERIENCE YOUR HAPPY REGARDING THE CIRCUMSTANCE YOU STAND IN NEED FOR BREAKTHROUGH. Are you ready to experience YOUR HAPPY? Say it with me... READY, SET... GO! Hannah had entered into the temple to have a talk and ENCOUNTER WITH GOD. She was given a WORD through the man of God ELI that she was going to GET what she needed to feel fulfilled. NO MATTER WHAT you need to do to get to your HAPPY, you are going to have to POSITION YOURSELF TO RECEIVE THE MANIFESTATION OF WHAT YOU ARE EXPECTING. HANNAH positioned herself to receive

The FIRST thing you are going to have to do to position yourself to experience YOUR HAPPY, you are going to have GET READY!

Points to Ponder

I. Decide that God's way is the only way

HANNAH got a word and it was confirmed by the man of God. That is all she needed. Her way wasn't working and when she went into the TEMPLE she made up her mind to do it God's way. Your way isn't working.. decide to handle it God's way. Yes, you can look in the magazine. Yes, you can get advise from your sister-friend. BUT God's way is the best way!!!

2. Refuse to resort to your old techniques of handling the circumstances in your life.

Find a Truth to stand on for your decision. Allow that Truth (word of God) to guide you on your journey.

3. Have trust and confidence in God's ability

Once you find your truth for your journey to HAPPY... trust that word to be the guide you need for purpose. If it is health, you know that God's wants you to be healthy. You body is how he fulfills his purpose through you. Don't allow temptations to pull you out of what the word says will be if you stick with him.

4. Develop a Plan

Don't just "wing it". Be purposeful. Write out your goal and the expectations. Give yourself a deadline. Find someone to hold you accountable. Maybe a sister--friend has the same goal; work together with her.

5. Be REALISTIC

There is a difference between long term and short term goals. Don't get so caught up in the end result that you forget to take the small steps necessary to reach your destination.

6. Watch your Company

You need people around you to support your decisions. Don't let people...who don't want your goal... to assist you on this journey. They will be a distraction and give you excuses not to follow through.

Questions

1. Are you happy?

2. What is causing the void?

3. What resources can you use to help you through your process?

4. Who can support you through your journey to HAPPY?

DAY 22

When you align with your purpose you ACTIVATE the CALL and Blessings attached to it, you ELEVATE your LIFE and PURPOSE. You are strategically and purposefully positioning yourself to IMPACT the lives of those you are called to influence with your life. You are POSITIONED to HONOR God with your life and fulfill the PLANS He has for you. What a AWESOME season you are about to embark on!

What stands out to me in this Reflection?

_____
_____
_____
_____

What do I need to Change to Live this Fully?

_____
_____
_____
_____

How will I Live this Today?

_____
_____
_____
_____

What does this Reflection mean to Me?

_____
_____
_____
_____
_____
_____
_____

What is your Affirmation to Remind you to Live this Fully Today?

_____
_____
_____

DAY 23

Even though you can't change your past you can use the lessons learned to impact your future for the good! "All things work together for good...."

What stands out to me in this Reflection?

_____
_____
_____
_____

What do I need to Change to Live this Fully?

_____
_____
_____
_____

How will I Live this Today?

_____
_____
_____
_____

What does this Reflection mean to Me?

_____
_____
_____
_____
_____
_____
_____
_____

What is your Affirmation to Remind you to Live this Fully Today?

_____
_____
_____

DAY24

People do things based on its value in their lives. IF it is valuable they are CONSISTENT. Why? Because it is seen as necessary and IMPORTANT to their lives. What do your HABITS say about what you VALUE? Remember value has many levels. Where does God fit in? Where do you fit in?

What stands out to me in this Reflection?

_____
_____
_____
_____

What do I need to Change to Live this Fully?

_____
_____
_____
_____

How will I Live this Today?

_____
_____
_____
_____

What does this Reflection mean to Me?

_____
_____
_____
_____
_____
_____
_____
_____
_____

What is your Affirmation to Remind you to Live this Fully Today?

_____
_____
_____

DAY 25

INVEST in YOURSELF in order to CHANGE your LIFE. 1. You NEED information. 2. INFORMATION comes through MENTORS 3. They have been where you are and have what you NEED. These CONNECTIONS will POSITION you for your BREAKTHROUGH

What stands out to me in this Reflection?

_____
_____
_____
_____

What do I need to Change to Live this Fully?

_____
_____
_____
_____

How will I Live this Today?

_____
_____
_____
_____

What does this Reflection mean to Me?

_____
_____
_____
_____
_____
_____
_____
_____

What is your Affirmation to Remind you to Live this Fully Today?

_____
_____
_____

DAY 26

TRANSITION isn't easy. You are being DEVELOPED and CHANGED. Like the butterfly your whole system has ton CHANGE and then BREAKOUT of the SHELL (remains) of who he USE to be but the results are AWESOME. Just like the butterfly PRESS...WIGGLE....STRETCH.... DONT GIVE UP... You are almost there.

What stands out to me in this Reflection?
_____
_____
_____
_____

What do I need to Change to Live this Fully?
_____
_____
_____
_____

How will I Live this Today?
_____
_____
_____
_____

What does this Reflection mean to Me?
_____
_____
_____
_____
_____
_____
_____
_____

What is your Affirmation to Remind you to Live this Fully Today?
_____
_____
_____

DAY 27

When you decide to Lift up the Standard in your life, you must learn to move. You must grab hold to your season of transition so you can advance to your next season.

What stands out to me in this Reflection?

_____
_____
_____
_____

What do I need to Change to Live this Fully?

_____
_____
_____
_____

How will I Live this Today?

_____
_____
_____
_____

What does this Reflection mean to Me?

_____
_____
_____
_____
_____
_____
_____
_____

What is your Affirmation to Remind you to Live this Fully Today?

_____
_____
_____

DAY 28

Your decisions should direct you not your EMOTIONS. Your emotions were
created to support your decisions.

What stands out to me in this Reflection?

_____
_____
_____
_____

What do I need to Change to Live this Fully?

_____
_____
_____
_____

How will I Live this Today?

_____
_____
_____
_____

What does this Reflection mean to Me?

_____
_____
_____
_____
_____
_____
_____
_____

What is your Affirmation to Remind you to Live this Fully Today?

_____
_____
_____

WEEKLY REVIEW

THIS WEEK:

NEXT WEEK:

2 **FAVORITE MEMORIES**

2 **WAYS I CAN HELP OTHERS**

3 **PLACES I WANT TO GO**

3 **THINGS I'M GRATEFUL FOR**

1 **THING I WANT TO GET BETTER AT**

1 **HARD LESSON LEARNED**

2 **THINGS I AM LOOKING FORWARD TO**

1 **THING I DID THIS WEEK I'M PROUD OF**

3 **NEW THINGS I WANT TO TRY**

WEEK 5

WHERE AM I NOW?

First, rate from 0 to 10 how much you believe each of the following statements. 0 means you completely disbelieve it. 10 means you think it is completely true.

I am a worthwhile person
I am as valuable as a person as anyone else
I have the qualities I need to live well
I don't feel like a overall failure
I can laugh at myself
I am happy to be me
I like myself, even when others reject me
I love and support myself, regardless of what happens
I am generally satisfied with the way I am developing as a person.
I respect myself
I'd rather be me than someone else
When I look into my eyes in the mirror I have a pleasant feeling

PERSONAL REFLECTION

_____
_____
_____
_____
_____
_____
_____
_____
_____

WEEKLY SELF REFLECTION

THIS WEEK I CAN

I NEED TO IMPROVE

MY GOAL THIS WEEK IS

WAYS TO REACH MY GOAL

1.

2.

3.

4.

5.

WEEKLY ACCOUNTABILITY

HEALTHY CHOICES

_____
_____
_____
_____
_____
_____
_____
_____
_____
_____
_____

ACCOUNTABILITY

Wake Time   _____
Quiet Time   _____
Exercise   _____
Power Time   _____
Bed Time   _____

IMPORTANT THINGS TO DO

_____
_____
_____
_____
_____
_____
_____
_____
_____
_____
_____
_____
_____
_____
_____

CALLS

_____
_____
_____
_____
_____
_____
_____
_____

I AM

TRUTHS

I AM is about declaring NOW who you are irregardless of if it is manifested. We SPEAK to BECOME.

What wisdom, scripture, poem, or declaration are you standing on.

1.

2.

3.

4.

5.

6.

7.

8.

9.

10.

VISION BOARD

Add and Draw picture(s) to keep before your eyes that you want manifested in your life.

WEEKLY SELF CARE PLAN

A Self Care Plan is about things you do for yourself. We are always giving out to others and you need to also give to yourself. How we express in action to others, should come from a place of "love" for yourself. You can't give what you don't have to give.

S	M	T	W	T	F	S

S	M	T	W	T	F	S

S	M	T	W	T	F	S

S	M	T	W	T	F	S

S	M	T	W	T	F	S

S	M	T	W	T	F	S

S	M	T	W	T	F	S

New Mind

There must be a shift. You must allow your old man mindset to pass away and renew your mind by conforming to truth. Your definition of who you are depends on it. When you release your old way of thinking it must be replaced with new thoughts and understanding. When you try to live by principles that haven't become life to you, it is just words that carry no weight or meaning in your lives. You haven't allowed truth to "convince" you through understanding that living what you believe will work. Romans 12:2 says, "that you may prove", you can't prove anything you don't understand. Understanding is the most powerful element in changing your lifestyle in conformity with truth for your journey.

You don't have to depend on your past, worldly standards, sister-friend advice, soap operas, horoscopes, magazines or anything that brings glory to self and not glory to God, to get change in your life. You must remove your "influence" from your lives and restore the covenant connection with God. You must become dependent on your new way of living. You must "see" your old lifestyle as contaminated and dangerous to your new directive. Lot's wife was not convinced! She didn't have understanding that the past was no longer apart of her future. Her attempt to "hold on" to her past cost her her life. It stopped her from moving forward towards her destiny and purpose. You are CALLED to REFLECT the GLORY of God in the earth. In order to do this you must allow new truths in your life. These truths will SHIFT YOU and you will begin to see the MANIFESTATION in your lives.

Points to Ponder

1. Don't allow the good of your past to dictate your obedience to God.
2. Obey what you know is true.
3. Close down "voices" that go contrary to your relationship with God.
4. Make up your mind to shift.
5. Lift up the VALUE of the Word in your life.
6. You must UNDERSTAND what you are applying to your life, don't function blindly.
7. Put in STUDY and REFLECTION time regarding your new MINDSET.
8. Ask YOURSELF WHY you believe what you believe and ANSWER the question.

Questions

1. What in your past is holding on to you?

2. What has been the hardest thing to release from your worldly life?

3. What does it do for you?

DAY 29

Your actions are testimonies of what you believe is acceptable behavior even if you say something else.

What stands out to me in this Reflection?

_____
_____
_____
_____

What do I need to Change to Live this Fully?

_____
_____
_____
_____

How will I Live this Today?

_____
_____
_____
_____

What does this Reflection mean to Me?

_____
_____
_____
_____
_____
_____
_____
_____

What is your Affirmation to Remind you to Live this Fully Today?

_____
_____
_____

DAY 30

Live every day on a fresh new start. Don't be held back by what happened yesterday, the day before, the week before, the year before, and so on.

What stands out to me in this Reflection?

_____
_____
_____
_____

What do I need to Change to Live this Fully?

_____
_____
_____
_____

How will I Live this Today?

_____
_____
_____
_____

What does this Reflection mean to Me?

_____
_____
_____
_____
_____
_____
_____
_____
_____

What is your Affirmation to Remind you to Live this Fully Today?

_____
_____
_____

30 DAY REVIEW

2 FAVORITE MEMORIES

2 WAYS I CAN HELP OTHERS

3 THINGS I'M GRATEFUL

3 PLACES I WANT TO GO

1 THING I WANT TO GET BETTER AT

1 HARD LESSON LEARNED

2 THINGS I AM LOOKING FORWARD TO

1 THING I DID THIS WEEK I'M PROUD OF

3 NEW THINGS I WANT TO TRY

MONTH

SUNDAY	MONDAY	TUESDAY	WEDNESDAY	THURSDAY	FRIDAY	SATURDAY

NOTES

_____

_____

_____

_____

_____

_____

_____

_____

MONTHLY GOAL PLAN

What is your vision for this month. When we write our vision it helps us bring focus. When you have focus you can get clarity about the steps necessary to move

1

		1
		2
		3

1	2	3	4	5	6	7	8	9	10	11	12	13	14	15
16	17	18	19	20	21	22	23	24	25	26	27	27	29	30

Goal   Action Steps

2

		1
		2
		3

1	2	3	4	5	6	7	8	9	10	11	12	13	14	15
16	17	18	19	20	21	22	23	24	25	26	27	27	29	30

Goal   Action Steps

3

		1
		2
		3

1	2	3	4	5	6	7	8	9	10	11	12	13	14	15
16	17	18	19	20	21	22	23	24	25	26	27	27	29	30

DAY 31

The past is a learning opportunity. You use it and find the lesson that will empower your future. When you don't find the lesson, you dwell on your past circumstances as failures and if you see your past as a success you can dwell to the point you don't believe you can do better.

What stands out to me in this Reflection?

_____
_____
_____
_____

What do I need to Change to Live this Fully?

_____
_____
_____
_____

How will I Live this Today?

_____
_____
_____
_____

What does this Reflection mean to Me?

_____
_____
_____
_____
_____
_____
_____
_____

What is your Affirmation to Remind you to Live this Fully Today?

_____
_____
_____

DAY 32

Quit complaining. Don't be the person that always says what is wrong and never does anything to change it. Stop complaining about your problems and work on them instead. Complaining is a reflection of someone who doesn't feel they are in control of their circumstance.

What stands out to me in this Reflection?

_____
_____
_____
_____

What do I need to Change to Live this Fully?

_____
_____
_____
_____

How will I Live this Today?

_____
_____
_____
_____

What does this Reflection mean to Me?

_____
_____
_____
_____
_____
_____
_____
_____

What is your Affirmation to Remind you to Live this Fully Today?

_____
_____
_____

DAY 33

Look at your circumstance and pray, find the truth you are going to stand on for the situation. Make that truth a active part of your mindset, heart and implement the principles regarding your circumstance

What stands out to me in this Reflection?

_____
_____
_____
_____

What do I need to Change to Live this Fully?

_____
_____
_____
_____

How will I Live this Today?

_____
_____
_____
_____

What does this Reflection mean to Me?

_____
_____
_____
_____
_____
_____
_____
_____

What is your Affirmation to Remind you to Live this Fully Today?

_____
_____
_____

DAY 34

Be proactive. Stop waiting for others around you to do something instead of take action yourself.

What stands out to me in this Reflection?

_____
_____
_____
_____

What do I need to Change to Live this Fully?

_____
_____
_____
_____

How will I Live this Today?

_____
_____
_____
_____

What does this Reflection mean to Me?

_____
_____
_____
_____
_____
_____
_____
_____
_____

What is your Affirmation to Remind you to Live this Fully Today?

_____
_____
_____

DAY 35

We must learn to take responsibility for our lives. This begins by taking responsibility for what IS your responsibility. We are quick to place our responsibility. Where do you fit in? What should you be doing? Remember we walk inharmony with God for our lives.

What stands out to me in this Reflection?

_____
_____
_____
_____

What do I need to Change to Live this Fully?

_____
_____
_____
_____

How will I Live this Today?

_____
_____
_____
_____

What does this Reflection mean to Me?

_____
_____
_____
_____
_____
_____
_____
_____

What is your Affirmation to Remind you to Live this Fully Today?

_____
_____
_____

WEEKLY REVIEW

THIS WEEK:

2 FAVORITE MEMORIES

3 THINGS I'M GRATEFUL FOR

1 HARD LESSON LEARNED

1 THING I DID THIS WEEK I'M PROUD OF

NEXT WEEK:

2 WAYS I CAN HELP OTHERS

3 PLACES I WANT TO GO

1 THING I WANT TO GET BETTER AT

2 THINGS I AM LOOKING FORWARD TO

3 NEW THINGS I WANT TO TRY

WEEK 6

WHERE AM I NOW?

First, rate from 0 to 10 how much you believe each of the following statements. 0 means you completely disbelieve it. 10 means you think it is completely true.

I believe I can change
My emotions are out of control
It is not my fault that I am emotional
I know what my triggers are but it is not my fault
It is easy for me to focus when circumstances are hard
I like trying new things
I am insecure
I am suppose to help people
I know the roots of my problems

PERSONAL REFLECTION

_____
_____
_____
_____
_____
_____
_____
_____
_____

WEEKLY SELF REFLECTION

THIS WEEK I CAN

I NEED TO IMPROVE

MY GOAL THIS WEEK IS

WAYS TO REACH MY GOAL

1.

2.

3.

4.

5.

WEEKLY ACCOUNTABILITY

HEALTHY CHOICES

_____
_____
_____
_____
_____
_____
_____
_____
_____
_____
_____

ACCOUNTABILITY

Wake Time _____
Quiet Time _____
Exercise _____
Power Time _____
Bed Time _____
_____

IMPORTANT THINGS TO DO

_____
_____
_____
_____
_____
_____
_____
_____
_____
_____
_____
_____
_____
_____
_____
_____

CALLS

_____
_____
_____
_____
_____
_____
_____

I AM

TRUTHS

I AM is about declaring NOW who you are irregardless of if it is manifested. We SPEAK to BECOME.

What wisdom, scripture, poem, or declaration are you standing on.

1.

2.

3.

4.

5.

6.

7.

8.

9.

10.

_____

_____

_____

_____

_____

_____

_____

VISION BOARD

Add and Draw picture(s) to keep before your eyes that you want manifested in your life.

WEEKLY SELF CARE PLAN

A Self Care Plan is about things you do for yourself. We are always giving out to others and you need to also give to yourself. How we express in action to others, should come from a place of "love" for yourself. You can't give what you don't have to give.

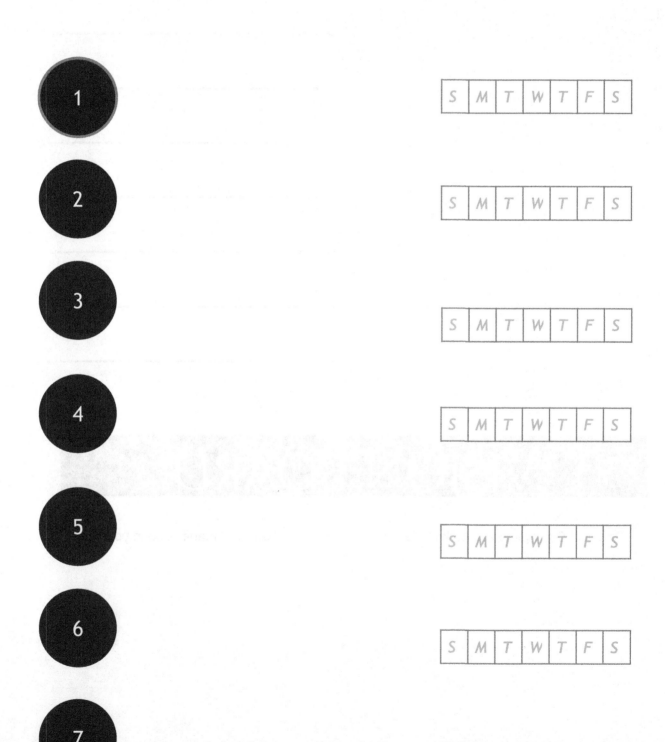

1 | S | M | T | W | T | F | S

2 | S | M | T | W | T | F | S

3 | S | M | T | W | T | F | S

4 | S | M | T | W | T | F | S

5 | S | M | T | W | T | F | S

6 | S | M | T | W | T | F | S

7 | S | M | T | W | T | F | S

Soul Clarity Reflection

Who Are You?

How many times have I heard this statement, "It's just the way that I am!?" Every time someone says this to me, they always try to be confident, but their body language speaks insecurity. Why?because they know they DON'T HAVE to act that way. IMAGE is not just how you look. Even if what you are doing, you feel is wrong. It is still ACCEPTABLE to you because you are doing it. Ouch! A lot of times you can allow LIFE to dictate how you respond to it. But as a KINGDOM WOMAN you are in control of your ATTITUDE and how you EXPRESS your opinion or reactions to life. It is hard for people to grasp that how they ACT is the TRUE REFLECTION of their beliefs and values, even tho they SAY something different. Your ACTIONS are the TRUE TESTIMONIES of your beliefs and values. It is what you use to handle life. Yes, you believe God's word. Yes, you know that it is true. BUT, YES you are doing something different.

Your beliefs are the laws and spiritual truths that you use to formulate your values. Your values are the "boundaries" of your life, that you use to make decisions regarding what you are to say and do regarding the circumstances that you face. Your CHARACTER or CHARACTERISTICS are the "behavioral" expressions that you have that other people can identify. For example, When you are angry, you frown. That is a Characteristic that is identifiable, so people know that you are mad. I know I am repeating myself, but it is necessary for you to understand. All of these (belief, values, characteristics/ behavior) are connected to your ATTITUDE. Your attitude is the "mentality" or the "justification" that you attribute to what you do. It is the "FEELING" you express to others. If you are nasty to someone one, your beliefs, values and behavior have given you PERMISSION to "act" that way or have the ATTITUDE that expresses nastiness. Your ATTITUDE, how you "express feeling

Points to Ponder

1. **Why do you act that way?**

You can not say, "I don't know". You must identify the root in order to break the cycle. It can be hurtful, but your PURPOSE and DESTINY depends on you identifying it. You are missing out on great relationships. You are keeping yourself from living. This "ATTITUDE" is blocking your FLOW and keeping you from people, places and experiences designed to take you to your next level.

2. **Yesterday is NOT today.**

You must learn to approach every circumstance with a open perspective. Let each circumstance stand on it's own merit. Don't limit yourself.

3. **What are you PROTECTING or NOT wanting to EXPERIENCE.**

You need to stop making excuses not to GROW. Yes, I said it right, GROW. Change is about GROWTH. Many people don't want to see the truth about themselves and they block the change with an "inappropriate" attitude regarding the circumstance. Your attitude covers many areas. It is a "PROTECTION" regarding not wanting to deal with things. It's not just about being nasty. IT'S a WALL to SHIELD you from experiences.

    a. You could have a ATTITUDE of fear.. not wanting to try new things...

    b. You could have a ATTITUDE of doubt.. not trusting...

    c. You could have a ATTITUDE of pouting... pretending to be insecure and baby... so people wont' require anything of you.

    d. You could have a ATTITUDE of quitting...

instead of working on something... you quit when it isn't PERFECT... or JUST like you want it.

    e. You could have a ATTITUDE of complaining.. something is always wrong.

    f. You could have a ATTITUDE of sarcasm.. you put people or things down.. you are a smart mouth.

Each of these ATTITUDES have roots! You must find the source of the ATTITUDE. You are EXPRESSING your PAST, a hurt or INSECURITY. You are not reflecting the beliefs, values and character of God. It is keeping you away from your next level. For many of us it is not the devil... It is US! Whether you fear being hurt or you are reacting "unconsciously" to your past. You MUST release it. When you Identify it and then Release it by FAITH so the POSSIBILITIES of walking into your purpose are made available to you. You release it by "DOING THE OPPOSITE".If you don't know what your ATTITUDE Reflections are ask someone you trust. They know and see it.

DAY 36

Focus on change. Don't think about things you can't change (namely what has happened and thoughts of other people) or unhappy things because these are disempowering. Instead focus on the things you can take action upon. That's the most constructive thing you can do in any situation.

What stands out to me in this Reflection?

_____
_____
_____
_____

What do I need to Change to Live this Fully?

_____
_____
_____
_____

How will I Live this Today?

_____
_____
_____
_____

What does this Reflection mean to Me?

_____
_____
_____
_____
_____
_____
_____
_____

What is your Affirmation to Remind you to Live this Fully Today?

_____
_____
_____

DAY 37

Stop focusing on what you can't change or what is out of your realm of influence. It can hinder forward movement because it is not within your capacity to change. Position yourself with action, become constructive in what you focus on and submit the issues that depend on others actions to God

What stands out to me in this Reflection?

_____
_____
_____
_____

What do I need to Change to Live this Fully?

_____
_____
_____
_____

How will I Live this Today?

_____
_____
_____
_____

What does this Reflection mean to Me?

_____
_____
_____
_____
_____
_____
_____
_____

What is your Affirmation to Remind you to Live this Fully Today?

_____
_____
_____

DAY 38

Focus on WHAT vs. How. Focus on WHAT you want first, before you think about HOW to do it. Anything is possible, as long as you set your mind, heart and soul to it.

What stands out to me in this Reflection?

_____
_____
_____
_____

What do I need to Change to Live this Fully?

_____
_____
_____
_____

How will I Live this Today?

_____
_____
_____
_____

What does this Reflection mean to Me?

_____
_____
_____
_____
_____
_____
_____
_____

What is your Affirmation to Remind you to Live this Fully Today?

_____
_____
_____

DAY 39

It is so easy to negate a great idea or dream by focusing solely on how something will get done. You end up discounting what is in our ability to do because you are solely looking at the end result or big picture. Remember ANYTHING is possible. You must set you mind, heart and will to see it come to pass. A elephant can be eaten, but only one bite at a time. Work on what is at your hand, allowing it to be the foundation for you next step.

What stands out to me in this Reflection?

_____
_____
_____
_____

What do I need to Change to Live this Fully?

_____
_____
_____
_____

How will I Live this Today?

_____
_____
_____
_____

What does this Reflection mean to Me?

_____
_____
_____
_____
_____
_____
_____
_____

What is your Affirmation to Remind you to Live this Fully Today?

_____
_____
_____

DAY 40

Create your own opportunities. You can wait for opportunities to drop in life.
Or you can go out there and create your own opportunities. The latter is
definite and much more empowering

What stands out to me in this Reflection?

_____
_____
_____
_____

What do I need to Change to Live this Fully?

_____
_____
_____
_____

How will I Live this Today?

_____
_____
_____
_____

What does this Reflection mean to Me?

_____
_____
_____
_____
_____
_____
_____
_____

What is your Affirmation to Remind you to Live this Fully Today?

_____
_____
_____

DAY 41

Step into the game! God has put limitless potential, purpose, and value inside of you. You are the initiator in your life. Be open to the process. Don't depend on others to give you permission to step out. You have what you need. The things you don't have, avail yourself to leaders, mentors, coaches, and spiritual leaders who can help you walk out the process

What stands out to me in this Reflection?

_____
_____
_____
_____

What do I need to Change to Live this Fully?

_____
_____
_____
_____

How will I Live this Today?

_____
_____
_____
_____

What does this Reflection mean to Me?

_____
_____
_____
_____
_____
_____
_____
_____

What is your Affirmation to Remind you to Live this Fully Today?

_____
_____
_____

DAY 42

Live more consciously each day. Stop sleepwalking through life. Your life is something to be experienced.

What stands out to me in this Reflection?

_____
_____
_____
_____

What do I need to Change to Live this Fully?

_____
_____
_____
_____

How will I Live this Today?

_____
_____
_____
_____

What does this Reflection mean to Me?

_____
_____
_____
_____
_____
_____
_____
_____

What is your Affirmation to Remind you to Live this Fully Today?

_____
_____
_____

WEEKLY REVIEW

THIS WEEK:

NEXT WEEK:

2 FAVORITE MEMORIES

2 WAYS I CAN HELP OTHERS

3 PLACES I WANT TO GO

3 THINGS I'M GRATEFUL FOR

1 THING I WANT TO GET BETTER AT

1 HARD LESSON LEARNED

2 THINGS I AM LOOKING FORWARD TO

1 THING I DID THIS WEEK I'M PROUD OF

3 NEW THINGS I WANT TO TRY

WEEK 7

WHERE AM I NOW?

First, rate from 0 to 10 how much you believe each of the following statements. 0 means you completely disbelieve it. 10 means you think it is completely true.

I settle for what I don't want so I can have peace

I resent people for who they treat me

People treat me well

People use me and don't ask how I feel

I tell people the truth about how I feel

I feel trapped in unhealthy relationships

I can forgive

I believe people should apologize before I forgive them

If I don't think about the problems in my life I will be fine

I speak my mind

PERSONAL REFLECTION

_____

_____

_____

_____

_____

_____

_____

_____

WEEKLY SELF REFLECTION

THIS WEEK I CAN

I NEED TO IMPROVE

MY GOAL THIS WEEK IS

WAYS TO REACH MY GOAL

1.

2.

3.

4.

5.

WEEKLY ACCOUNTABILITY

HEALTHY CHOICES

_____
_____
_____
_____
_____
_____
_____
_____
_____
_____
_____

ACCOUNTABILITY

Wake Time _____
Quiet Time _____
Exercise _____
Power Time _____
Bed Time _____
_____

IMPORTANT THINGS TO DO

_____
_____
_____
_____
_____
_____
_____
_____
_____
_____
_____
_____
_____
_____
_____

CALLS

_____
_____
_____
_____
_____
_____

I AM

TRUTHS

I AM is about declaring NOW who you are irregardless of if it is manifested. We SPEAK to BECOME.

What wisdom, scripture, poem, or declaration are you standing on.

1.

2.

3.

4.

5.

6.

7.

8.

9.

10.

VISION BOARD

Add and Draw picture(s) to keep before your eyes that you want manifested in your life.

WEEKLY SELF CARE PLAN

A Self Care Plan is about things you do for yourself. We are always giving out to others and you need to also give to yourself. How we express in action to others, should come from a place of "love" for yourself. You can't give what you don't have to give.

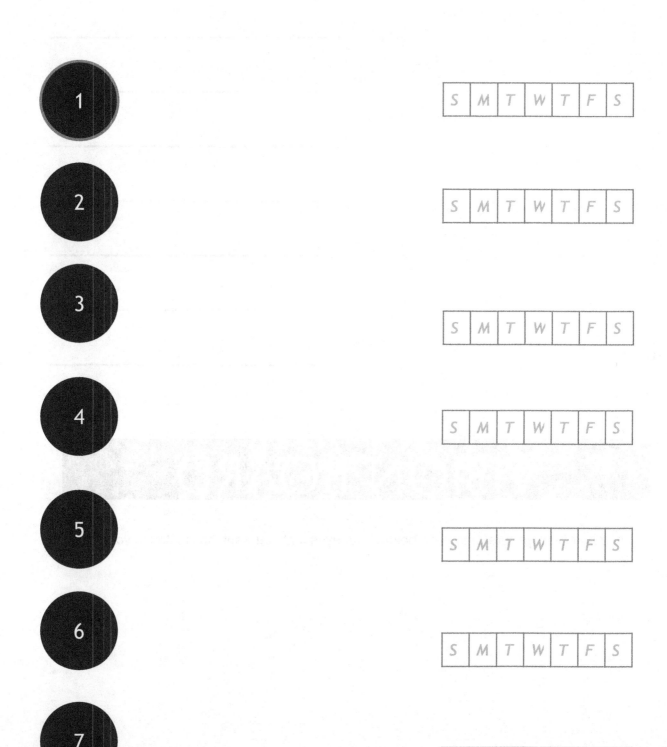

| 1 | | S | M | T | W | T | F | S |

| 2 | | S | M | T | W | T | F | S |

| 3 | | S | M | T | W | T | F | S |

| 4 | | S | M | T | W | T | F | S |

| 5 | | S | M | T | W | T | F | S |

| 6 | | S | M | T | W | T | F | S |

| 7 | | S | M | T | W | T | F | S |

Don't Settle

Leah was married to a man who was tricked into a relationship with her. Because she allowed her father and husband's perspective of her to define her worth; she missed out on God's view of her. Each child she had became a reflection of her struggle with her self worth and her desire to be wanted by her husband.

She never truly saw God's love and desire upon her life. Even in the midst of her challenges and negative self perception, he continued to bless her with children. Instead of seeing the blessing as a reflection of God's love for her, she twisted it as an opportunity to prove to her husband and Rachel that she was valuable.

Our definition of ourselves seeps into our lives. We can not hide it. It shows in our conversation. It shows in our dress. It shows in how we relate to the people in our lives. It is a product of our past and for some our present situation. It has caused damage to our SELF VALUE and WORTH and we must change it. There must be healing from the past in order to make good, quality decisions about our future. Otherwise, our decisions will be contaminated and clouded by what has shaped us. This includes how we apply and perceive the impact of the WORD of God on our lives. Because Leah had low self esteem and value she SETTLED for what she got; a husband that did not love her and a father who did not value her for who she was as a person and daughter.

It is easy for us (women) to SETTLE. We know how to "pretend" everything is o.k. when it is not. We know how to put OURSELVES on the back burner for other people. We know how to "live" (if you can call it that) day to day reducing our desires and wants in our lives. Today I say, STOP settling. You are powerful, beautiful and wanted. God has a DIVINE DESIGN for your life and womanhood. He desires you to be WHOLE and healthy (spiritually, emotionally and naturally). But it begins with you.

Leah missed the blessing that was right in front of her because she didn't make the decision that she was WORTH IT! She didn't see the hand of God on her life. She didn't see the hand of God regarding her children. She didn't see the blessings that were being given because she didn't know her WORTH! Her worth became the product of being accepted by a man who didn't value her. Her worth was wrapped up in trying to prove to her sister that she was valuable! Her worth was about proving that she was a better wife than Rachel. She never became valuable to herself!!!!!

You must become valuable to yourself in order not to SETTLE. It begins with understanding that you have a purpose. You have a reason for being here. You are God's BEST!
SAY it with me... I AM GOD'S BEST! I AM VALUABLE!... I AM WORTH IT! I DESERVE THE BEST!!!!!

Points to Ponder

1. Decide you want to heal.

What has happened in your past that has brought brokenness to your self value and worth?. Was it a missing parent? A Broken Marriage? A unhealthy friendship? Betrayal? It can be difficult but you must be willing to look at the circumstance in order to heal. If you don't know what it is, ask the Holy Spirit to reveal it to you.

2. Begin with forgiveness.

Forgiveness is for you, not for the one who has caused you harm. When you forgive you are saying that you no longer hold the other person hostage to the circumstance. You will no longer punish them for what has happened. You are deciding to move on. That is easier said than done. The truth is they are living their life and not thinking about what has happened to you. You are mad and they are shopping. Release YOURSELF to move forward!

3. Speak LIFE to yourself!

Speak what God says about you. Let your words be positive and self building. Learn to accept compliments. Don't tell people you bought that outfit 10 years ago, when they say you look good!!! Say THANK YOU! Compliment yourself. Keep your mind focused on the positive about yourself. As you allow the healing process to begin... you will increase your self value and worth and you will see yourself moving into your destiny.

Questions

1. What has happened in your past that you need to heal from?

2. What are you going to confess over you life and circumstance?

3. Who do you need to forgive? Why?

DAY 43

Be active spirit, soul and body in your life. You can do this by moving from existing to LIVING. You were given dominion. Live, make the decisions you need to shape your direction. Your life is suppose to follow your decisions not lead them.

What stands out to me in this Reflection?

_____

_____

_____

_____

What do I need to Change to Live this Fully?

_____

_____

_____

_____

How will I Live this Today?

_____

_____

_____

_____

What does this Reflection mean to Me?

_____

_____

_____

_____

_____

_____

_____

_____

What is your Affirmation to Remind you to Live this Fully Today?

_____

_____

_____

DAY 44

Be committed to your growth. The richer your life experience the higher your consciousness and understanding. This comes from your commitment to growth.

What stands out to me in this Reflection?

_____
_____
_____
_____

What do I need to Change to Live this Fully?

_____
_____
_____
_____

How will I Live this Today?

_____
_____
_____
_____

What does this Reflection mean to Me?

_____
_____
_____
_____
_____
_____
_____
_____

What is your Affirmation to Remind you to Live this Fully Today?

_____
_____
_____

DAY 45

KNOW YOURSELF. This means knowing who you are and what you represent. Be clear of your personal identity.

What stands out to me in this Reflection?

_____
_____
_____
_____

What do I need to Change to Live this Fully?

_____
_____
_____
_____

How will I Live this Today?

_____
_____
_____
_____

What does this Reflection mean to Me?

_____
_____
_____
_____
_____
_____
_____
_____

What is your Affirmation to Remind you to Live this Fully Today?

_____
_____
_____

DAY 46

You must know yourself in order to discover your purpose. What do you believe? Is it your truth or information you believe is true? Are you implementing it in your life? Are you living authentically or is your circumstances determining your journey.

What stands out to me in this Reflection?

_____
_____
_____
_____

What do I need to Change to Live this Fully?

_____
_____
_____
_____

How will I Live this Today?

_____
_____
_____
_____

What does this Reflection mean to Me?

_____
_____
_____
_____
_____
_____
_____
_____

What is your Affirmation to Remind you to Live this Fully Today?

_____
_____
_____

DAY 47

You must know yourself in order to discover your purpose. What do you believe? Is it your truth or information you believe is true? Are you implementing it in your life? Are you living authentically or is your circumstances determining your journey.

What stands out to me in this Reflection?

_____
_____
_____
_____

What do I need to Change to Live this Fully?

_____
_____
_____
_____

How will I Live this Today?

_____
_____
_____
_____

What does this Reflection mean to Me?

_____
_____
_____
_____
_____
_____
_____
_____

What is your Affirmation to Remind you to Live this Fully Today?

_____
_____
_____

DAY 48

Discover your life purpose. Set the mission statement for your life; one that
will drive you to life your life to the fullest.

What stands out to me in this Reflection?

_____
_____
_____
_____

What do I need to Change to Live this Fully?

_____
_____
_____
_____

How will I Live this Today?

_____
_____
_____
_____

What does this Reflection mean to Me?

_____
_____
_____
_____
_____
_____
_____
_____
_____

What is your Affirmation to Remind you to Live this Fully Today?

_____
_____
_____

DAY 49

Everyone must be actively seeking and developing their purpose. It is not a take it or leave it decision. You are here for a reason. Your life is to reflect God in the earth. You are suppose to be living in a way that develops that truth or purpose and allow God to use your life as a reflection of him in the lives of others. Your life is the tool God uses to express his glory in the earth. There is something unique and individual about you that is here to bring a uniqueness for impact your life.

What stands out to me in this Reflection?

_____

_____

_____

_____

What do I need to Change to Live this Fully?

_____

_____

_____

_____

How will I Live this Today?

_____

_____

_____

_____

What does this Reflection mean to Me?

_____

_____

_____

_____

_____

_____

_____

_____

What is your Affirmation to Remind you to Live this Fully Today?

_____

_____

_____

WEEK 8

WHERE AM I NOW?

First, rate from 0 to 10 how much you believe each of the following statements. 0 means you completely disbelieve it. 10 means you think it is completely true.

I know my truth
I change what I believe based on the situation
I faithfully live my truth
I share my truth with others
I am living authentically
I wear a "mask" depending on who I am talking too
People don't know the real me
I live true to myself
I am courageous
I am myself no matter who is around

PERSONAL REFLECTION

_____
_____
_____
_____
_____
_____
_____
_____

WEEKLY SELF REFLECTION

THIS WEEK I CAN

I NEED TO IMPROVE

MY GOAL THIS WEEK IS

WAYS TO REACH MY GOAL

1.

2.

3.

4.

5.

WEEKLY ACCOUNTABILITY

HEALTHY CHOICES

_____
_____
_____
_____
_____
_____
_____
_____
_____
_____
_____

ACCOUNTABILITY

Wake Time _____
Quiet Time _____
Exercise _____
Power Time _____
Bed Time _____
_____

IMPORTANT THINGS TO DO

_____
_____
_____
_____
_____
_____
_____
_____
_____
_____
_____
_____
_____
_____

CALLS

_____
_____
_____
_____
_____
_____
_____
_____

I AM

TRUTHS

I AM is about declaring NOW who you are irregardless of if it is manifested. We SPEAK to BECOME.

What wisdom, scripture, poem, or declaration are you standing on.

1.

2.

3.

4.

5.

6.

7.

8.

9.

10.

_____

_____

_____

_____

_____

_____

_____

VISION BOARD

Add and Draw picture(s) to keep before your eyes that you want manifested in your life.

WEEKLY SELF CARE PLAN

A Self Care Plan is about things you do for yourself. We are always giving out to others and you need to also give to yourself. How we express in action to others, should come from a place of "love" for yourself. You can't give what you don't have to give.

S	M	T	W	T	F	S

S	M	T	W	T	F	S

S	M	T	W	T	F	S

S	M	T	W	T	F	S

S	M	T	W	T	F	S

S	M	T	W	T	F	S

S	M	T	W	T	F	S

Soul Clarity Reflection

What is your Truth

TRUTH means **FIDELITY** to a required standard; the state or quality of being FAITHFUL to; a system of concepts that REFLECTS a perspective. It sounds like a easy question, but it isn't that simple. A lot of women think that if you say you believe something, then that is your truth. In reality, your truth is what you FAITHFULLY use in your circumstances to get RESULTS. It is your IMMEDIATE response. It is the concepts and understanding that you depend on to resolve the issues you are facing in your life. It is the PILLARS that you depend on in REACTION to your circumstances. Your truth is your GO TO perspective! So even tho you believe that the word is TRUTH, you must ASK yourself if you are USING that TRUTH for your circumstances. If you are not using the TRUTH of the WORD as your RESPONSE to the circumstances you face... You need to ask yourself what are you using and WHY?

What is your response to someone getting you ANGRY?

What is your response to someone cutting in LINE?

What is your response to someone CURSING at you?

What is your response to CONFLICT?

How do you respond to a man FLIRTING with you.. and you are married?

This is not just about NEGATIVE responses in your circumstances but it is also your POSITIVE responses. What do they reflect. What is your TRUTH with regards to POSITIVE circumstances?

Do you put the cart back at the grocery store?

Why do you do what you do? Why do you respond the way you respond? Did you ever analyze the FOUNDATION to your reaction? You must be deliberate regarding THE TRUTH . You are to make the truth of the word of God your truth for your life. You must be SURE. You can't move back and forth between the ways of your flesh (old man) and the word. I love when the scripture says, "chance gusts of teaching and wavering." The TRUTH that you live in needs to be founded on the word of God. Anything else is "chance gusts!" The bible sees TRUTHS not founded on the word as "erratic blowing winds" that takes us in all kinds of directions. These TRUTHS that are not founded on the word are seen as "fickle", "unreliable", "happen-stance". You don't want your decisions to be "CIRCUMSTANTIAL" like a "gambler engaged" in a game. You want your TRUTH to be the GUIDING force that DEFINES who you are and WHAT you stand for!!! You as a Kingdom Woman are a reflection of something greater than yourself. You are a reflection of the truth of the word of God in the earth, functioning to bring Glory to GOD!.

Points to Ponder

1. Your life MUST become PURPOSEFUL!

You can not live where CIRCUMSTANCES blow you back and forth. Your TRUTH must become what CONTROLS your CIRCUMSTANCE. God wants your life to "LOVINGLY" express TRUTH in ALL THINGS. The word says SPEAKING, DEALING, LIVING TRULY. The word says when you do... you are "growing up in every way". So the word of God says that LIVING a LIFE of TRUTH means that you are becoming MATURE BELIEVERS.

This week ANALYZE your TRUTHS and what is guiding your decisions for your circumstance. Begin to remove the truth of your flesh and replace it with the truth of the word. PRACTICE living out those truths this week and watch the hand of God move mightily in your life.

DAY 50

You should be living your truth so your life can reflect your truth. You need to know your truth and begin living it in every area of your life. You should be exhausting your potential and leaving the earth empty.

What stands out to me in this Reflection?

_____
_____
_____
_____

What do I need to Change to Live this Fully?

_____
_____
_____
_____

How will I Live this Today?

_____
_____
_____
_____

What does this Reflection mean to Me?

_____
_____
_____
_____
_____
_____
_____
_____

What is your Affirmation to Remind you to Live this Fully Today?

_____
_____
_____

DAY 51

What do you believe? Define your beliefs? You need to know it in order to live your best life. What adages and principles do you want to follow in your life?

What stands out to me in this Reflection?

_____
_____
_____
_____

What do I need to Change to Live this Fully?

_____
_____
_____
_____

How will I Live this Today?

_____
_____
_____
_____

What does this Reflection mean to Me?

_____
_____
_____
_____
_____
_____
_____
_____

What is your Affirmation to Remind you to Live this Fully Today?

_____
_____
_____

DAY 52

What are your truths. They impact the decisions you make daily and even a minute by minute basis. Your truth is a fundamental part of your identity. It is the blueprint that shapes your values. Your values are the framework for your decisions and your decision are the expression of who you are that is identifiable to others. But it begins with you taking the time to form and investigate the truths your life sits upon for your journey.

What stands out to me in this Reflection?

_____
_____
_____
_____

What do I need to Change to Live this Fully?

_____
_____
_____
_____

How will I Live this Today?

_____
_____
_____
_____

What does this Reflection mean to Me?

_____
_____
_____
_____
_____
_____
_____
_____

What is your Affirmation to Remind you to Live this Fully Today?

_____
_____
_____

DAY 53

You can not live as hypocrites to what you say you believe is true. You must be diligent, study, understand and be able to implement with your actions your truth. Your actions are the expression of what you believe, consciously or unconsciously. You are responsible to live it with or without a audience. If you only live what you believe is true in front of other it isn't your truth.

What stands out to me in this Reflection?

_____
_____
_____
_____

What do I need to Change to Live this Fully?

_____
_____
_____
_____

How will I Live this Today?

_____
_____
_____
_____

What does this Reflection mean to Me?

_____
_____
_____
_____
_____
_____
_____
_____

What is your Affirmation to Remind you to Live this Fully Today?

_____
_____
_____

DAY 54

There is a vision in your heart for your life. Don't be scared of it. It is there for a reason, there is knowledge and counsel to discover it and make it come to pass.

What stands out to me in this Reflection?

_____
_____
_____
_____

What do I need to Change to Live this Fully?

_____
_____
_____
_____

How will I Live this Today?

_____
_____
_____
_____

What does this Reflection mean to Me?

_____
_____
_____
_____
_____
_____
_____
_____

What is your Affirmation to Remind you to Live this Fully Today?

_____
_____
_____

DAY 55

Stop putting your life on hold. Are you putting any parts of your life on hold?
What is one area of your life you have been putting off/avoiding/denying?
Uncover it and start working on it.

What stands out to me in this Reflection?

_____
_____
_____
_____

What do I need to Change to Live this Fully?

_____
_____
_____
_____

How will I Live this Today?

_____
_____
_____
_____

What does this Reflection mean to Me?

_____
_____
_____
_____
_____
_____
_____
_____

What is your Affirmation to Remind you to Live this Fully Today?

_____
_____
_____

DAY 56

Live in alignment with your purpose. What can you start doing immediately that will let you live 100% in alignment with your purpose? How can you live true to your purpose within every context/situation/environment you are in every second of the day?

What stands out to me in this Reflection?

_____
_____
_____
_____

What do I need to Change to Live this Fully?

_____
_____
_____
_____

How will I Live this Today?

_____
_____
_____
_____

What does this Reflection mean to Me?

_____
_____
_____
_____
_____
_____
_____
_____

What is your Affirmation to Remind you to Live this Fully Today?

_____
_____
_____

WEEKLY REVIEW

THIS WEEK:

NEXT WEEK:

2 **FAVORITE MEMORIES**

2 **WAYS I CAN HELP OTHERS**

3 **PLACES I WANT TO GO**

3 **THINGS I'M GRATEFUL FOR**

1 **THING I WANT TO GET BETTER AT**

1 **HARD LESSON LEARNED**

2 **THINGS I AM LOOKING FORWARD TO**

1 **THING I DID THIS WEEK I'M PROUD OF**

3 **NEW THINGS I WANT TO TRY**

WEEK 9

WHERE AM I NOW?

First, rate from 0 to 10 how much you believe each of the following statements. 0 means you completely disbelieve it. 10 means you think it is completely true.

My emotions are under control
I am living my purpose
I am easily distracted
I am growing
It is easy for me to live my truth when circumstances are hard

PERSONAL REFLECTION

_____
_____
_____
_____
_____
_____
_____
_____
_____

WEEKLY SELF REFLECTION

THIS WEEK I CAN

I NEED TO IMPROVE

MY GOAL THIS WEEK IS

WAYS TO REACH MY GOAL

1.

2.

3.

4.

5.

WEEKLY ACCOUNTABILITY

HEALTHY CHOICES

_____
_____
_____
_____
_____
_____
_____
_____
_____
_____
_____

ACCOUNTABILITY

Wake Time _____
Quiet Time _____
Exercise _____
Power Time _____
Bed Time _____
_____

IMPORTANT THINGS TO DO

_____
_____
_____
_____
_____
_____
_____
_____
_____
_____
_____
_____
_____
_____
_____

CALLS

_____
_____
_____
_____
_____
_____
_____
_____

I AM

I AM is about declaring NOW who you are irregardless of if it is manifested. We SPEAK to BECOME.

1.

2.

3.

4.

5.

6.

7.

8.

9.

10.

TRUTHS

What wisdom, scripture, poem, or declaration are you standing on.

_____

_____

_____

_____

_____

_____

_____

VISION BOARD

Add and Draw picture(s) to keep before your eyes that you want manifested in your life.

WEEKLY SELF CARE PLAN

A Self Care Plan is about things you do for yourself. We are always giving out to others and you need to also give to yourself. How we express in action to others, should come from a place of "love" for yourself. You can't give what you don't have to give.

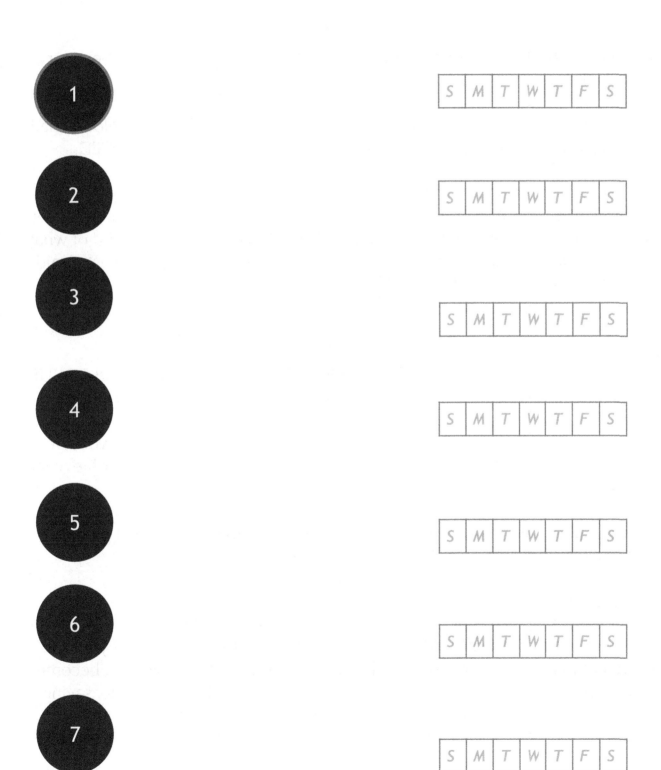

What is True

TRUE means **REAL, AUTHENTIC, SINCERE, FIRM,** in allegiance, loyal, being or reflecting the essential or genuine character of something.

Do you remember the song, "I Shall Not, I Shall Not be Moved, I Shall Not, I Shall Not be Moved, Just like a tree planted by the waters, I Shall Not Be MOVED.

That is what it means to be AUTHENTIC or TRUE. You are so convinced with where you stand, you are not moved! Last week we talked about TRUTH. It means being FAITHFUL to standards or a way of being. Well, TRUTH is the "reflection" of what is TRUE. What are you reflecting? What are you "expressing?" Again, like we said last week, then THAT IS YOUR TRUTH.

WHAT IS TRUE?

In order to LIVE as a AUTHENTIC KINGDOM WOMAN, the word of God is TRUE. It is the foundation for what you believe and value. It is the STANDARD for your life. You are FAITHFUL or living in TRUTH to it. It doesn't matter what the "world" lives by. Even if it sounds good and "works", it is not "your" TRUTH that you live TRUE to. You are not to be moved. The word is the STANDARD for your life, even if you don't always understand why.

You live your life under the "sovereignty" of God and know that He will give you enlightenment for where you lack understanding.

IT'S A TESTIMONY

In order to LIVE AUTHENTIC you can not just "say" the right thing. The "right thing" must become the "TESTIMONY" of your life. If it is not the testimony of your life, you are not living as sincere and genuine as you could or should be. You become a example of being double minded. This can lead to living like a hypocrite, saying one thing and living something else. That sounds 'harsh", but it is true and very easy to do.

Points to Ponder

1. MEDITATE

You have to study, concentrate, pay attention to the word of God in order for it to become the foundation of our TRUTH. It must become TRUE to you. You must use it to replace the areas of your life that go contrary to it.

2. PROCESS

You must get understanding. The word says that in all the knowledge that you have access to, you must understand it. It doesn't have "true" value in your life until you can use it to help you discern what is going on in your life.

3. ACT

Even tho this text is about someone "discerning" someone who is dangerous... you can become and many times ARE the woman with loose lips dripping or the one with bitter and sharp words.

When you are not living AUTHENTIC, you are living two lives and the BATTLE is not with someone else, it is with you.

It begins with you. You must first be TRUE to YOURSELF. You must first "VALUE" your own TRUTH and you show that you value your own TRUTH by 'living it".

It is time! Proverbs 5:6 talks about the woman who has lost her way for her LIFE. She doesn't have direction and is "aimless".

God is moving you to higher depths in HIM! The AUTHENTIC LIFE is available. You will become a Kingdom Woman who lives a REAL, GENUINE life reflecting the Character of God in the earth for your Womanhood Journey through His TRUTH and what is TRUE for our lives.

.

DAY 57

Every minute of your life you should be actively moving forward. You can do something to be forward progressing. If you are not in a season of implementation, then maybe you are in a season of building the blueprint or closing out one season to enter another. There is something you can be doing. Remember that your life today is a reflection of yesterday's preparation, and today is preparation for your future

What stands out to me in this Reflection?

_____
_____
_____
_____

What do I need to Change to Live this Fully?

_____
_____
_____
_____

How will I Live this Today?

_____
_____
_____
_____

What does this Reflection mean to Me?

_____
_____
_____
_____
_____
_____
_____
_____

What is your Affirmation to Remind you to Live this Fully Today?

_____
_____
_____

DAY 58

Don't do things for the sake of doing them. Always evaluate what you're doing and only do it if there is meaning behind them. Don't be afraid to quit the things that don't serve your path

What stands out to me in this Reflection?

_____
_____
_____
_____

What do I need to Change to Live this Fully?

_____
_____
_____
_____

How will I Live this Today?

_____
_____
_____
_____

What does this Reflection mean to Me?

_____
_____
_____
_____
_____
_____
_____
_____

What is your Affirmation to Remind you to Live this Fully Today?

_____
_____
_____

DAY 59

Do the things you love, because life is too precious to spend it doing anything else. If you don't enjoy something, then don't do it. Spend your time and energy on things that bring you fulfillment and happiness.

What stands out to me in this Reflection?

_____
_____
_____
_____

What do I need to Change to Live this Fully?

_____
_____
_____
_____

How will I Live this Today?

_____
_____
_____
_____

What does this Reflection mean to Me?

_____
_____
_____
_____
_____
_____
_____
_____

What is your Affirmation to Remind you to Live this Fully Today?

_____
_____
_____

DAY 60

Learn from criticism. Be open to criticism but don't be affected by it. Criticism is meant to help you be a better person. You must change how you receive it. It highlights areas in our lives we must improve so we can move forward.

What stands out to me in this Reflection?
_____
_____
_____
_____

What do I need to Change to Live this Fully?
_____
_____
_____
_____

How will I Live this Today?
_____
_____
_____
_____

What does this Reflection mean to Me?
_____
_____
_____
_____
_____
_____
_____
_____

What is your Affirmation to Remind you to Live this Fully Today?
_____
_____
_____

30 DAY REVIEW

2 FAVORITE MEMORIES

2 WAYS I CAN HELP OTHERS

3 THINGS I'M GRATEFUL

3 PLACES I WANT TO GO

1 THING I WANT TO GET BETTER AT

1 HARD LESSON LEARNED

2 THINGS I AM LOOKING FORWARD TO

1 THING I DID THIS WEEK I'M PROUD OF

3 NEW THINGS I WANT TO TRY

MONTH

SUNDAY	MONDAY	TUESDAY	WEDNESDAY	THURSDAY	FRIDAY	SATURDAY

_____

_____

_____

_____

_____

_____

_____

_____

MONTHLY GOAL PLAN

What is your vision for this month. When we write our vision it helps us bring focus. When you have focus you can get clarity about the steps necessary to move

1

	1	
	2	
	3	

1	2	3	4	5	6	7	8	9	10	11	12	13	14	15
16	17	18	19	20	21	22	23	24	25	26	27	27	29	30

Goal   Action Steps

2

	1	
	2	
	3	

1	2	3	4	5	6	7	8	9	10	11	12	13	14	15
16	17	18	19	20	21	22	23	24	25	26	27	27	29	30

Goal   Action Steps

3

	1	
	2	
	3	

1	2	3	4	5	6	7	8	9	10	11	12	13	14	15
16	17	18	19	20	21	22	23	24	25	26	27	27	29	30

DAY 61

Don't badmouth other people. If there's anything you don't like about someone, say it to him/her in the face – otherwise, don't say it at all. It's not nice to do that. Our words have life and they return as a reflection in our lives.

What stands out to me in this Reflection?

_____
_____
_____
_____

What do I need to Change to Live this Fully?

_____
_____
_____
_____

How will I Live this Today?

_____
_____
_____
_____

What does this Reflection mean to Me?

_____
_____
_____
_____
_____
_____
_____
_____

What is your Affirmation to Remind you to Live this Fully Today?

_____
_____
_____

DAY 62

Believe in yourself and your abilities. Remove your limiting beliefs and replace them with empowering ones

What stands out to me in this Reflection?

_____
_____
_____
_____

What do I need to Change to Live this Fully?

_____
_____
_____
_____

How will I Live this Today?

_____
_____
_____
_____

What does this Reflection mean to Me?

_____
_____
_____
_____
_____
_____
_____
_____

What is your Affirmation to Remind you to Live this Fully Today?

_____
_____
_____

DAY 63

Let go of your unhappy past. This includes past grievances, heartbreaks, sadness,disappointments, etc. Forgive those who may have done you wrong in the past.

What stands out to me in this Reflection?

_____
_____
_____
_____

What do I need to Change to Live this Fully?

_____
_____
_____
_____

How will I Live this Today?

_____
_____
_____
_____

What does this Reflection mean to Me?

_____
_____
_____
_____
_____
_____
_____
_____

What is your Affirmation to Remind you to Live this Fully Today?

_____
_____
_____

WEEKLY REVIEW

THIS WEEK:

NEXT WEEK:

2 **FAVORITE MEMORIES**

2 **WAYS I CAN HELP OTHERS**

3 **PLACES I WANT TO GO**

3 **THINGS I'M GRATEFUL FOR**

1 **THING I WANT TO GET BETTER AT**

1 **HARD LESSON LEARNED**

2 **THINGS I AM LOOKING FORWARD TO**

1 **THING I DID THIS WEEK I'M PROUD OF**

3 **NEW THINGS I WANT TO TRY**

WEEK 10

WHERE AM I NOW?

First, rate from 0 to 10 how much you believe each of the following statements. 0 means you completely disbelieve it. 10 means you think it is completely true.

Its hard for me to focus on the big picture
I am easily influenced by others regarding how i feel
I am distracted by the emotions of others
I can name my values
It is easy for me to focus when circumstances are hard
I can be happy no matter what
I resort to my old habits after deciding to act differently
I am aware of what is going on around me
It is God's responsibility to make me happy
I can only be happy when things are good

PERSONAL REFLECTION

_____
_____
_____
_____
_____
_____
_____
_____

WEEKLY SELF REFLECTION

THIS WEEK I CAN

I NEED TO IMPROVE

MY GOAL THIS WEEK IS

WAYS TO REACH MY GOAL

1.

2.

3.

4.

5.

WEEKLY ACCOUNTABILITY

HEALTHY CHOICES

_____
_____
_____
_____
_____
_____
_____
_____
_____
_____
_____

ACCOUNTABILITY

Wake Time   _____
Quiet Time   _____
Exercise   _____
Power Time   _____
Bed Time   _____
_____

IMPORTANT THINGS TO DO

_____
_____
_____
_____
_____
_____
_____
_____
_____
_____
_____
_____
_____
_____
_____

CALLS

_____
_____
_____
_____
_____
_____
_____
_____

I AM

I AM is about declaring NOW who you are irregardless of if it is manifested. We SPEAK to BECOME.

1.

2.

3.

4.

5.

6.

7.

8.

9.

10.

TRUTHS

What wisdom, scripture, poem, or declaration are you standing on.

_____

_____

_____

_____

_____

_____

_____

VISION BOARD

Add and Draw picture(s) to keep before your eyes that you want manifested in your life.

WEEKLY SELF CARE PLAN

A Self Care Plan is about things you do for yourself. We are always giving out to others and you need to also give to yourself. How we express in action to others, should come from a place of "love" for yourself. You can't give what you don't have to give.

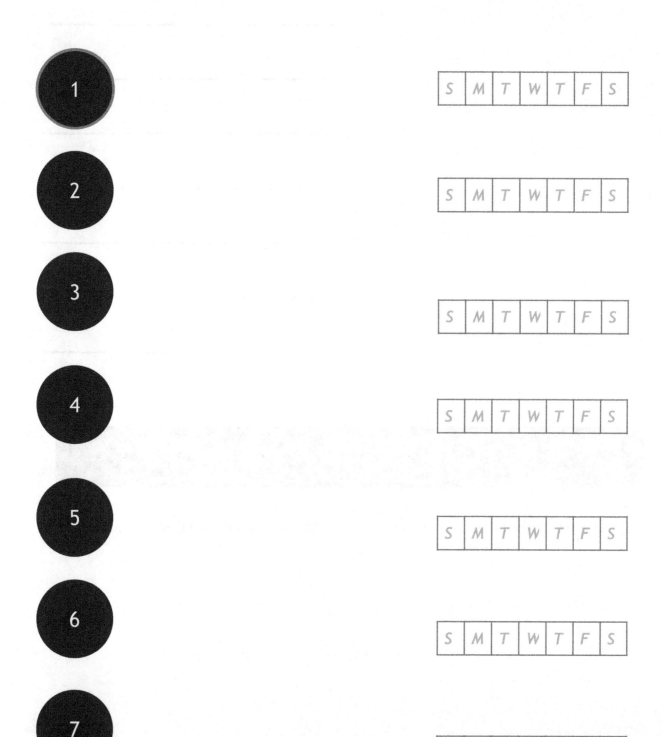

1 | S | M | T | W | T | F | S |

2 | S | M | T | W | T | F | S |

3 | S | M | T | W | T | F | S |

4 | S | M | T | W | T | F | S |

5 | S | M | T | W | T | F | S |

6 | S | M | T | W | T | F | S |

7 | S | M | T | W | T | F | S |

Soul Clarity Reflection

Look at the Big Picture

There are consequences to every choice you make, especially as Leaders and Examples. Before you make choices you must ask yourself if you are willing to deal with the consequences. You can forget that you are not always in control of the outcome of a circumstance. Consequences can not always be calculated. You don't always get the reaction you expect. People are not always in the place you thought.

If David killed Nabal it could have disrupted his succession to the throne. It could have even bore fruit in his own heart. Remember David was going to murder Nabal and destroy all his possessions. *"But those things that proceeds out of the mouth comes from the heart, and they defile a man. For out of the heart proceeds evil thoughts, murders, adulteries, fornications, thefts, false witness, blasphemies. These are the things which defile a man..."* **Matthew 15:18-20.**

YOU IMPACT OTHERS
He was not at war with Nabal. He just didn't like Nabal's reaction to his request. David wasn't thinking about how this would affect his army, to go and slaughter an innocent family. David was considered their ruler. David chose to justify his actions with a lie. He convinced himself that he was owed something. *"If a ruler pays attention to lies, all his servants become wicked"* **Proverbs 29:12** There is only one who knows the future and we are to trust his word for our direction. **Proverbs 3:5 says, *"Trust in the Lord with all your heart, and lean not on your own understanding, in all your ways acknowledge Him, and He shall direct your paths.***

A PLACE OF STABILITY
How many times have you reacted without looking at the "big picture"? In my own life the consequences were more than I could have imagined in some circumstances. There must be a place of stability when you make choices regarding your circumstance. Stability says that you are secure to put "weight" on something. Before you sit in a chair you touch it to see if it is stable.

As a KINGDOM WOMAN your stability is found in the principles of the word. When you deal with the word KINGDOM you are saying that you do things according to God's terms. His terms are found in the word. **Isaiah 33:6 says, *"Wisdom and knowledge will be the stability of your times, and the strength of salvation; the fear of the Lord is His treasure.*** As you look at the "big picture" His word must be the source of our decision.

Leaders and Examples lead. Are you out of control? Do others have more authority over your life than you do? It is something to analyze and be honest about regarding how our emotions have been given the "right" to direct our lives.

Power Points

1. DON'T LEAD WITH EMOTIONS As a Leader and Example you must not allow your emotions to distract from the "big picture". Emotions were meant to *confirm and support* a decision. They were not meant to be the *reason* for the decision. As you know emotions can change from one minute to the next. **Proverbs 29:11 says, "A fool vents all his feelings, but a wise man holds them back.** David's emotions were leading him to murder someone who was not legally obligated to him. David quickly came to himself after hearing Abigail's analysis of the circumstance. He complimented her and said she gave him "good judgment".

2. YOU MUST USE GOOD JUDGMENT As a Leader and Example you should never be so emotional that you loose perspective. You are in control of yourself. To many people are blaming others for their emotional outburst, negative attitudes and are not taking personal accountability. I can't tell you the number of times I have heard women say, "If they wouldn't have done that, I wouldn't have acted that way." That is a deception of the to justify being out of control. You must acknowledge that you act out to get a particular outcome. Yelling forces other to acknowledge our point of view. You don't want to admit it but you believe it works because you might do it often.

3. THE POWER OF WORDS As a Leader and Example you must be mindful of your words. They are not easily retracted. Many use words like, I don't *feel* like it so I won't go. You curse because you believe it gets the reactions you want. Pouting makes others feel sorry for you and YES you get something out of it! When you think this way you are allowing outside forces to regulate your actions.

4. ARE YOU OUT OF CONTROL As a Leader and Example you lead. Are you out of control? Do others have more authority over your life than you do? It is something to analyze and be honest about regarding how our emotions have been given the "right" to direct our lives.

As a KINGDOM WOMAN you understand that it is not just about you. You understand that there is more than one solution to a problem. Your way isn't always the best way. Others have a right to their opinion without you feeling violated or disrespected because people don't see your point of view. You are NOT regulated by others actions, emotions, outburst or ignorance. You are in control of yourself. There is more at stake than you getting your way. You must think about the future. You must think about others and you must rely on the truth.

DAY 64

If it doesn't support where you are going then it is a distraction. We are living a life of purpose...which means our relationships, activities, connections, daily routines support that purpose.

What stands out to me in this Reflection?

_____
_____
_____
_____

What do I need to Change to Live this Fully?

_____
_____
_____
_____

How will I Live this Today?

_____
_____
_____
_____

What does this Reflection mean to Me?

_____
_____
_____
_____
_____
_____
_____
_____

What is your Affirmation to Remind you to Live this Fully Today?

_____
_____
_____

DAY 65

Try new things. What's something you'd normally not do? Get out of your comfort zone and try something different.

What stands out to me in this Reflection?
_____
_____
_____
_____

What do I need to Change to Live this Fully?
_____
_____
_____
_____

How will I Live this Today?
_____
_____
_____
_____

What does this Reflection mean to Me?
_____
_____
_____
_____
_____
_____
_____
_____

What is your Affirmation to Remind you to Live this Fully Today?
_____
_____
_____

DAY 66

You must Choose to REDEFINE your Life! It is a decision not a wish or fantasy. You have to make the decision for yourself. It doesn't matter when you begin, it's never to late to BECOME Who You Are Meant to Be! DECIDE it's time for change. Next week or Next Year is not going to be any easier. Each day has its own issues in it. You can not look to tomorrow as being the answer for today. Our today prepares us for tomorrow. There is NO better time than WHEN you DECIDE. Let me help. Join me and a community of like minded women who are on the SAME journey as you.

What stands out to me in this Reflection?

_____
_____
_____
_____

What do I need to Change to Live this Fully?

_____
_____
_____
_____

How will I Live this Today?

_____
_____
_____
_____

What does this Reflection mean to Me?

_____
_____
_____
_____
_____
_____
_____
_____

What is your Affirmation to Remind you to Live this Fully Today?

_____
_____
_____

DAY 67

You can no longer depend on broken truths as the support system for your identity and decisions. Today begins a new covenant with you and God. Begin to strip yourselves of your unrenewed self which includes your previous manners, habits and behaviors that are now corruption to where you are going. Why? Because who you were no longer supports where you are going. Who you are today, got you to where you are today. But now it is about who you need to become to get you where you are going. You must constantly renew your mind. It creates a fresh mental and spiritual attitude.

What stands out to me in this Reflection?

_____
_____
_____
_____

What do I need to Change to Live this Fully?

_____
_____
_____
_____

How will I Live this Today?

_____
_____
_____
_____

What does this Reflection mean to Me?

_____
_____
_____
_____
_____
_____
_____
_____

What is your Affirmation to Remind you to Live this Fully Today?

_____
_____
_____

DAY 68

Your destiny is not fate or chance. It is your active participation in your personal growth combined with God's divine plan to be glorified through your life. You make choices today that intentionally shape your future. In order to become who God has purposed you need FAITH and PERSONAL DEVELOPMENT. You personal development supports your purpose by developing your skills, talents, competencies, abilities and truth. You need both for success, otherwise there is no implementation and you live your life BELIEVING but never really experiencing BREAK THRU in your life.

What stands out to me in this Reflection?

_____
_____
_____
_____

What do I need to Change to Live this Fully?

_____
_____
_____
_____

How will I Live this Today?

_____
_____
_____
_____

What does this Reflection mean to Me?

_____
_____
_____
_____
_____
_____
_____
_____

What is your Affirmation to Remind you to Live this Fully Today?

_____
_____
_____

DAY 69

Being busy is not a correct "reader" for being effective. Busy doesn't mean you are bringing value to what you are doing. You sometimes compensate for not knowing your purpose by using physical activity to bring value into other peoples lives. You could truly be doing that by understanding what you bring to the table. What you have been given is designed to impact your realm of influence through your value. Being to busy should mean not as effective, too much on the plate, jack of all trades. You sometimes think it mean multi tasking. But when you are always" taking up the slack" for those in your realm of influence, instead of teaching, equipping, developing and empowering those you are "held" accountable to impact, your BUSY doesn't have the right meaning. What does your busy mean?

What stands out to me in this Reflection?

_____
_____
_____
_____

What do I need to Change to Live this Fully?

_____
_____
_____
_____

How will I Live this Today?

_____
_____
_____
_____

What does this Reflection mean to Me?

_____
_____
_____
_____
_____
_____
_____
_____

What is your Affirmation to Remind you to Live this Fully Today?

_____
_____
_____

DAY 70

You are called to bring your value into people's lives. Your value causes increase to take place in others not the replacement of their responsibility to their own lives. If they are not increased to where they can use those lessons that you have added, you are replacing them in the areas of responsibility and you are suppose to be empowering them by bringing your value into their lives for the development and empowerment of their purpose. You must understand what you bring into their lives by becoming your best self and through this process you learn your gifts, talents, abilities, attributes, strengths and impact.

What stands out to me in this Reflection?

_____
_____
_____
_____
_____

What do I need to Change to Live this Fully?

_____
_____
_____
_____
_____

How will I Live this Today?

_____
_____
_____
_____

What does this Reflection mean to Me?

_____
_____
_____
_____
_____
_____
_____
_____
_____

What is your Affirmation to Remind you to Live this Fully Today?

_____
_____
_____

WEEKLY REVIEW

THIS WEEK:

NEXT WEEK:

2 FAVORITE MEMORIES

2 WAYS I CAN HELP OTHERS

3 PLACES I WANT TO GO

3 THINGS I'M GRATEFUL FOR

1 THING I WANT TO GET BETTER AT

1 HARD LESSON LEARNED

2 THINGS I AM LOOKING FORWARD TO

1 THING I DID THIS WEEK I'M PROUD OF

3 NEW THINGS I WANT TO TRY

WEEK 11

WHERE AM I NOW?

First, rate from 0 to 10 how much you believe each of the following statements. 0 means you completely disbelieve it. 10 means you think it is completely true.

My circumstances determine if I am happy
I am easily influenced by others regarding how i feel
I am distracted by the emotions of others
I can name my values
It is easy for me to focus when circumstances are hard
I can be happy no matter what
I resort to my old habits after deciding to act differently
I am aware of what is going on around me
It is God's responsibility to make me happy
I can only be happy when things are good

PERSONAL REFLECTION

_____
_____
_____
_____
_____
_____
_____
_____

WEEKLY SELF REFLECTION

THIS WEEK I CAN

I NEED TO IMPROVE

MY GOAL THIS WEEK IS

WAYS TO REACH MY GOAL

1.

2.

3.

4.

5.

WEEKLY ACCOUNTABILITY

HEALTHY CHOICES

_____
_____
_____
_____
_____
_____
_____
_____
_____
_____

ACCOUNTABILITY

Wake Time   _____
Quiet Time   _____
Exercise   _____
Power Time   _____
Bed Time   _____
             _____

IMPORTANT THINGS TO DO

_____
_____
_____
_____
_____
_____
_____
_____
_____
_____
_____
_____
_____

CALLS

_____
_____
_____
_____
_____
_____
_____
_____

I AM

TRUTHS

I AM is about declaring NOW who you are irregardless of if it is manifested. We SPEAK to BECOME.

What wisdom, scripture, poem, or declaration are you standing on.

1.

2.

3.

4.

5.

6.

7.

8.

9.

10.

_____

_____

_____

_____

_____

_____

_____

VISION BOARD

Add and Draw picture(s) to keep before your eyes that you want manifested in your life.

WEEKLY SELF CARE PLAN

A Self Care Plan is about things you do for yourself. We are always giving out to others and you need to also give to yourself. How we express in action to others, should come from a place of "love" for yourself. You can't give what you don't have to give.

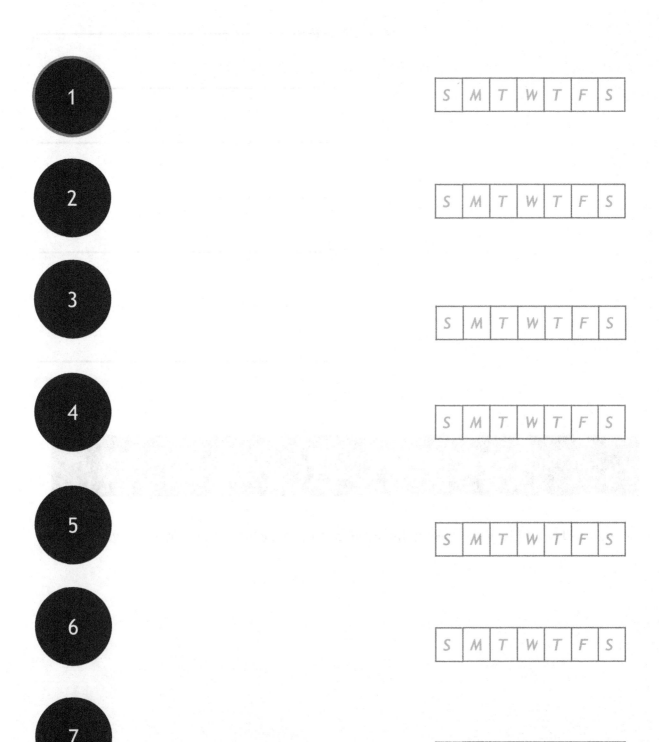

| 1 | | S | M | T | W | T | F | S |

| 2 | | S | M | T | W | T | F | S |

| 3 | | S | M | T | W | T | F | S |

| 4 | | S | M | T | W | T | F | S |

| 5 | | S | M | T | W | T | F | S |

| 6 | | S | M | T | W | T | F | S |

| 7 | | S | M | T | W | T | F | S |

Guard Your Heart

Be careful what you allow in your heart. Your beliefs, values, understanding and perspectives are found in your heart. The heart is considered your core. It is where you *store* the information you use to make decisions regarding the circumstances you face on a daily basis.

It is your gauge, what you use to decide if what you see, hear or experience is safe or acceptable to receive. Your heart holds your confirmed cautions. It is there to keep you safe from harm or danger. It protects, watches over and keeps what you receive (ears, eyes) under close watch in order to prevent escape or misconduct. This ONLY takes place when you purposefully guard your heart. In order to successfully guard your heart, you must have a foundation of truth which helps you decide what is acceptable or unacceptable information, which leads to acceptable or unacceptable words or deeds. God intended His word to be this foundation.

DON'T ALLOW IT IN YOUR SPACE
To many people allow all kinds of information in their space. They find themselves unconsciously being shaped by outside mediums (television, commercials, people, music) that has a truth that is sometimes contrary to the word of God. It is as easy as having the television on and doing something else. Or sleeping with the television or radio on and not realizing what is getting in your heart.

WHAT DEFINES YOU
If you are not careful people, companies, life, the enemy or EXPERIENCES will begin to define you and shape your heart. You will trust your flesh to give you counsel. *"But my people would not heed My voice, and Israel would have none of Me. So I gave them over to their own stubborn heart, to walk in their own counsel. Oh that my people would listen to Me, that Israel would walk in My ways!" Psalms 81:11-13*

THE MOST VALUABLE QUALIFIER
Remember as a KINGDOM WOMAN you believe that your actions are a reflection of your beliefs and values. Your actions and words are a glimpse into who you are. It is how you know what people are really like. It is only through modern times that you find it acceptable to speak one thing and believe something else. The most valuable qualifiers to another person's perspective (heart) are their words and actions. What you accept, justify and then act on in word or deed has its roots in our heart. ***"My mouth shall speak wisdom, and the meditation of my heart gives understanding." Psalms 49:3.***

Power Points

1. PUT LIFE AND EXPERIENCE IN IT'S PLACE Life and experiences are not suppose to define or shape your perspective outside of God's will for your life. Your life and experiences are to be opportunities to develop a Kingdom centered perspective and relationship with God.

2. IT'S AN OPPORTUNITY Each situation is an opportunity to bring you closer or push you further from your belief system and values. You should allow your experiences to move you to truth and the faithfulness of God.

3. IT'S FUNDAMENTAL The heart is a fundamental element for a KINGDOM WOMAN. It is a testimony to who you are and what you have accepted as your truth.

4. YOUR HEART SHINES THROUGH Your behavior shows others your mindset and what you believe is acceptable. You must press to reflect your truth. This can only be done when you are diligent to guard your hearts.

Remember you are here to be a glory to Him not yourself. You must be motivated by truth not flesh. You must believe that truth works. This comes through spending time in the truth and applying it daily to your life.

DAY 71

You are not a slave or accessory in everyone's life. You bring VALUE to those circumstances because you are VALUABLE. You contribute "worth". You bring gifts, talents, abilities, wisdom, truth, action to the table that can make other people's lives better. Therefore you don't "reduce" who you are to slave/accessory status". You must believe and appreciate yourself before others will. How you see yourself is reflected through your actions. When you neglect yourself you bring LESS value into the lives of your realm of influence because you without knowledge of who you are you can not express it through your life.

What stands out to me in this Reflection?

_____
_____
_____
_____

What do I need to Change to Live this Fully?

_____
_____
_____
_____

How will I Live this Today?

_____
_____
_____
_____

What does this Reflection mean to Me?

_____
_____
_____
_____
_____
_____
_____
_____

What is your Affirmation to Remind you to Live this Fully Today?

_____
_____
_____

DAY 72

There must be a shift. You must release your old mindset and renew your mind by conforming to the truths, principles, wisdom and information needed to move your process forward. Your Purpose depends on it. When you release your old way of thinking it must be replaced with new thoughts and understanding. You must begin to make them an active part of your daily lives. When you try to live by principles, wisdom and information that hasn't become life to us, it is just words that carry no weight or meaning in your life. You haven't allowed these truths, wisdom and information to "convince" you through understanding that living accordingly is necessary to your destiny and purpose.

What stands out to me in this Reflection?

_____
_____
_____
_____

What do I need to Change to Live this Fully?

_____
_____
_____
_____

How will I Live this Today?

_____
_____
_____
_____

What does this Reflection mean to Me?

_____
_____
_____
_____
_____
_____
_____
_____
_____

What is your Affirmation to Remind you to Live this Fully Today?

_____
_____
_____

DAY 73

You don't have to depend on your past, myths, sister-friend advice, soap operas, horoscopes, magazines or anything that is contrary to your belief system to position yourself to fulfill purpose in your life. You must remove their "influence" from your life and restore the connection with truths that support your belief system and values. Otherwise you will feel divided and question the choices you are making because you feel insecure in this "new arena" of living to manifest purpose in your life.

What stands out to me in this Reflection?

_____
_____
_____
_____

What do I need to Change to Live this Fully?

_____
_____
_____
_____

How will I Live this Today?

_____
_____
_____
_____

What does this Reflection mean to Me?

_____
_____
_____
_____
_____
_____
_____
_____

What is your Affirmation to Remind you to Live this Fully Today?

_____
_____
_____

DAY 74

Close down "voices" that go contrary to your purpose. You are in another season.
What worked for you in the past is not designed to help you go to your next level.
Who you were got you to where you are, but for who you need to become, there is
new wisdom, truths and information designed to impact your life.

What stands out to me in this Reflection?

_____
_____
_____
_____

What do I need to Change to Live this Fully?

_____
_____
_____
_____

How will I Live this Today?

_____
_____
_____
_____

What does this Reflection mean to Me?

_____
_____
_____
_____
_____
_____
_____
_____

What is your Affirmation to Remind you to Live this Fully Today?

_____
_____
_____

DAY 75

Without understanding your "why" you will always resort to what you feel comfortable doing. The wisdom, truths and information that you are adding to your life has to be more than words. You must UNDERSTAND what you are applying to your life. Don't function blindly, your heart know the difference. If you are not settled in your heart, you will not do it. Lift up the VALUE of this information in your life. Put in STUDY, MEDITATION and REFLECTION time regarding your new MINDSET. Ask YOURSELF WHY you believe what you believe and ANSWER the question. Don't take it lightly.

What stands out to me in this Reflection?

_____
_____
_____
_____

What do I need to Change to Live this Fully?

_____
_____
_____
_____

How will I Live this Today?

_____
_____
_____
_____

What does this Reflection mean to Me?

_____
_____
_____
_____
_____
_____
_____
_____

What is your Affirmation to Remind you to Live this Fully Today?

_____
_____
_____

DAY 76

Wha is your truth? It sounds like a easy question, but it isn't that simple. A lot of women think that if you say you believe something then that is your truth. In reality, your truth is what you FAITHFULLY use in your circumstances to get RESULTS. It is your IMMEDIATE response. It is the concepts and understanding that you depend on to resolve the issues you are facing in your life. It is the PILLARS that you depend on in REACTION to your circumstances.

What stands out to me in this Reflection?

_____
_____
_____
_____

What do I need to Change to Live this Fully?

_____
_____
_____
_____

How will I Live this Today?

_____
_____
_____
_____

What does this Reflection mean to Me?

_____
_____
_____
_____
_____
_____
_____
_____

What is your Affirmation to Remind you to Live this Fully Today?

_____
_____
_____

DAY 77

It is so easy to get comfortable. You find yourself just existing. You want more but unconsciously you know it will "require" something of you and you fall back into the routine. You find yourself not living with direction. You don't know your purpose. You don't know how to move forward. You don't know how to break the routine. When you set goals you give yourself a clear pathway towards a set destination. You will have something to aim for. It helps you set perimeters for your choices. It helps you make decisions about relationships and other things that will come up in your life. You don't have to do something GRAND. Begin small. Practice following through and you will begin to see yourself moving forward and accomplishing the things you set your hands to. It is a great feeling to accomplish what you have desired to come to pass in your life.

What stands out to me in this Reflection?
_____
_____
_____
_____

What do I need to Change to Live this Fully?
_____
_____
_____
_____

How will I Live this Today?
_____
_____
_____
_____

What does this Reflection mean to Me?
_____
_____
_____
_____
_____
_____
_____
_____

What is your Affirmation to Remind you to Live this Fully Today?
_____
_____
_____

WEEKLY REVIEW

THIS WEEK:

NEXT WEEK:

2 FAVORITE MEMORIES

2 WAYS I CAN HELP OTHERS

3 PLACES I WANT TO GO

3 THINGS I'M GRATEFUL FOR

1 THING I WANT TO GET BETTER AT

1 HARD LESSON LEARNED

2 THINGS I AM LOOKING FORWARD TO

1 THING I DID THIS WEEK I'M PROUD OF

3 NEW THINGS I WANT TO TRY

WEEK 12

WHERE AM I NOW?

First, rate from 0 to 10 how much you believe each of the following statements. 0 means you completely disbelieve it. 10 means you think it is completely true.

My circumstances determine if I am happy

I am easily influenced by others regarding how i feel

I am distracted by the emotions of others

I can name my values

It is easy for me to focus when circumstances are hard

I can be happy no matter what

I resort to my old habits after deciding to act differently

I am aware of what is going on around me

It is God's responsibility to make me happy

I can only be happy when things are good

PERSONAL REFLECTION

_____

_____

_____

_____

_____

_____

_____

_____

WEEKLY SELF REFLECTION

THIS WEEK I CAN

I NEED TO IMPROVE

MY GOAL THIS WEEK IS

WAYS TO REACH MY GOAL

1.

2.

3.

4.

5.

WEEKLY ACCOUNTABILITY

HEALTHY CHOICES

_____
_____
_____
_____
_____
_____
_____
_____
_____
_____
_____

ACCOUNTABILITY

Wake Time _____
Quiet Time _____
Exercise _____
Power Time _____
Bed Time _____
_____

IMPORTANT THINGS TO DO

_____
_____
_____
_____
_____
_____
_____
_____
_____
_____
_____
_____
_____
_____

CALLS

_____
_____
_____
_____
_____
_____
_____
_____

I AM

I AM is about declaring NOW who you are irregardless of if it is manifested. We SPEAK to BECOME.

1.

2.

3.

4.

5.

6.

7.

8.

9.

10.

TRUTHS

What wisdom, scripture, poem, or declaration are you standing on.

_____

_____

_____

_____

_____

_____

VISION BOARD

Add and Draw picture(s) to keep before your eyes that you want manifested in your life.

WEEKLY SELF CARE PLAN

A Self Care Plan is about things you do for yourself. We are always giving out to others and you need to also give to yourself. How we express in action to others, should come from a place of "love" for yourself. You can't give what you don't have to give.

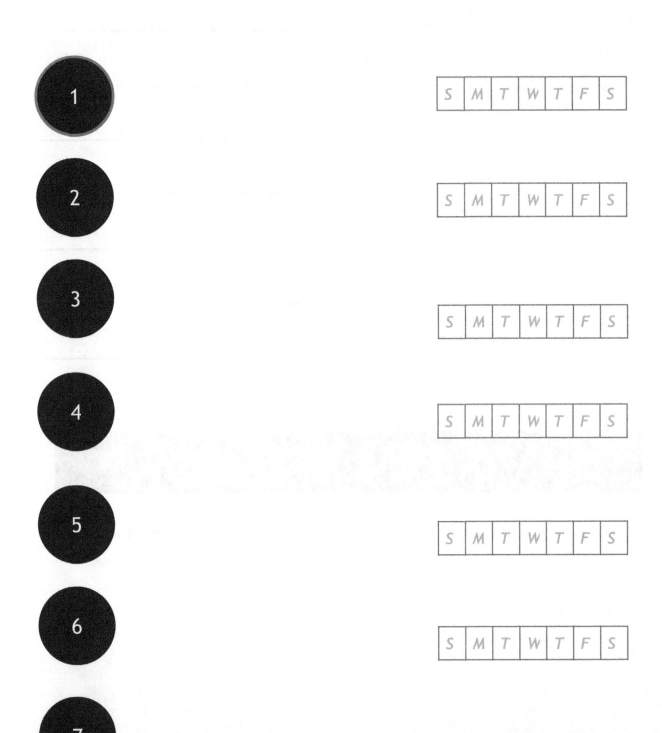

		S	M	T	W	T	F	S

1 — S M T W T F S

2 — S M T W T F S

3 — S M T W T F S

4 — S M T W T F S

5 — S M T W T F S

6 — S M T W T F S

7 — S M T W T F S

Accountability

We must stand with a unified front and agenda of empowerment and encouragement towards each other. God is calling us to IMPACT others for his GLORY, but in order to be effective we must learn about accountability and what is attached to it. ACCOUNTABILITY is one of the hardest things you will do. It means that you give someone else permission to hold you to your decisions and word. You also open yourself to correction.

 What powerful words. When we are not open to be accountable and corrected, we not only hinder ourselves but others. As leaders in our homes, jobs, relationships and communities, we are responsible for other people. When we refuse to be accountable, our choices reflect our ignorance and we use that "lack of understanding" in our decisions.

In order to benefit from Accountability, we must make sure that the person we are accountable to... we trust. You need to trust their judgment. You need to trust their motive. You need to trust that they want you to succeed. Otherwise, you will doubt their wisdom and advice when they share their perspective regarding your circumstance.

This falls in line with UNITY because EVERYONE *needs someone else in their life to be accountable too*. Yes, we try to be accountable to ourselves, but we can also release ourselves from our choices. We need someone else's eye and view of ourselves and our direction. In order to grow we need to be accountable to someone.

Points to Ponder

1. **YOU CAN'T WALK IN OFFENSE**. When you are easily offended, you are saying that someone else's opinion is a personal ATTACK on you. We must learn to separate ourselves from criticism, opinion or communication. It is the reception of INFORMATION.

2. **YOU NEEDS TO HEAR IT.** You need to hear someone else's opinion. The word says that there is safety in a multitude of counsel. If it is hard for you to hear someone else's opinion, there is healing that needs to take place in your life. You need to find the source of the "harm" and move forward.

3. **YOU NEED THE STRUCTURE**. Accountability brings healthy structure in our lives. It keeps us from living in a "dream world". When we live with structure, it gives us a framework to move forward.

4. **YOU NEED TO HEAL**. There are things in your life, you will not be able to see. It is like trying to give yourself a haircut. You will never do as good as someone who is standing and has a better viewpoint and perspective of your head. Healing begins with being able to SEE and HEAR the TRUTH. Until you are open, you will limit yourself.

5. **IT PREPARES YOU FOR THE FUTURE**. Accountability has a purpose. It helps you move your vision and purpose forward. It prepares you for what is coming in your life so you will reach your goals.

Accountability is something that the enemy and the flesh hates, but it is one of the KEYS to SUCCESS. It brings healing, direction and perspective for our lives. We need it. Don't run from accountability.

DAY 78

In order to LIVE AUTHENTIC you can not just "say" the right thing. The "right thing" must become the "TESTIMONY" of your life. If it is not the testimony of your life, you are not living as sincere and genuine as you could or should be. You become examples of being double minded. This can lead to living like a hypocrite, saying one thing and living something else. That sounds 'harsh", but it is true and very easy to do.

What stands out to me in this Reflection?

_____
_____
_____
_____

What do I need to Change to Live this Fully?

_____
_____
_____
_____

How will I Live this Today?

_____
_____
_____
_____

What does this Reflection mean to Me?

_____
_____
_____
_____
_____
_____
_____
_____

What is your Affirmation to Remind you to Live this Fully Today?

_____
_____
_____

DAY 79

In order to LIVE AUTHENTIC, you can not get comfortable "believing" but never transforming to what you say you believe. Many women never take the TIME to Meditate, Process, and Act on what is TRUE in their circumstances. You find ourselves living out of CONVENIENCE and not out of TRUTH and what is TRUE. You are not being PURPOSEFUL and end up just EXISTING.

What stands out to me in this Reflection?
_____
_____
_____
_____

What do I need to Change to Live this Fully?
_____
_____
_____
_____

How will I Live this Today?
_____
_____
_____
_____

What does this Reflection mean to Me?
_____
_____
_____
_____
_____
_____
_____
_____

What is your Affirmation to Remind you to Live this Fully Today?
_____
_____
_____

DAY 80

In order to LIVE AUTHENTIC, you must slow down and begin to evaluate your life. You must take each piece of your puzzle and put it into perspective with HOW you want to live. You must move beyond "DREAMING" about the great life and begin SETTING UP OUR LIVES so you can LIVE the life you desire to express. You truly can have it!! You can move your life from Glory to Glory!! You can see the manifestation of His word towards you. You can LIVE IT and not just "wish" that it will come to pass for us one day, yet in our heart not believe it. It can become a reality. Don't SETTLE on just "wishing". LIVE IT. Create a allegiance to it, allow it to be a "accurate formation or position in your life. You can live AUTHENTIC.

What stands out to me in this Reflection?
_____
_____
_____
_____

What do I need to Change to Live this Fully?
_____
_____
_____
_____

How will I Live this Today?
_____
_____
_____
_____

What does this Reflection mean to Me?
_____
_____
_____
_____
_____
_____
_____
_____

What is your Affirmation to Remind you to Live this Fully Today?
_____
_____
_____

DAY 81

In order to live in peace and happiness, you must be comfortable with yourself. You must STAND for what you believe and not shift and change to fit the mold of others. This doesn't mean that you are not flexible in your relationships and open to others ways of doing things. It means you are settled in your TRUTH, the foundation for your belief system. As a Kingdom Woman your TRUTH is based on the TRUE WORD, but you MUST live it OUT, so it develops and becomes a "sincere" expression! As the saying goes... "TO THY OWN-SELF BE TRUE"..

What stands out to me in this Reflection?

_____
_____
_____
_____

What do I need to Change to Live this Fully?

_____
_____
_____
_____

How will I Live this Today?

_____
_____
_____
_____

What does this Reflection mean to Me?

_____
_____
_____
_____
_____
_____
_____
_____

What is your Affirmation to Remind you to Live this Fully Today?

_____
_____
_____

DAY 82

EVERY ASPECT of your life is "groomed" by your VALUES. That is why VALUES are soooo important in the shaping of your future. They are yours, nobody can tell you what to place value on. You need to find them. HOW? You need to look for what triggers a very strong emotion in you (anger, love, hate, jealousy) there will probably be a link to a core value. Your CORE VALUES help you make better decisions and better choices. They guide you. They are your map and compass in your life. When you know your VALUES you can assess the different aspects of your life and DECIDE how you will move forward.

What stands out to me in this Reflection?

_____
_____
_____
_____

What do I need to Change to Live this Fully?

_____
_____
_____
_____

How will I Live this Today?

_____
_____
_____
_____

What does this Reflection mean to Me?

_____
_____
_____
_____
_____
_____
_____
_____

What is your Affirmation to Remind you to Live this Fully Today?

_____
_____
_____

DAY 83

Your values are the boundary keepers of your decisions. What is and isn't acceptable? Make sure your values are being represented in all your decisions. Sometimes you react with your flesh and not your values. It is something that you have accepted to handle the circumstance, but it is not within the context of what you hold dear through the word of God.

What stands out to me in this Reflection?

_____
_____
_____
_____

What do I need to Change to Live this Fully?

_____
_____
_____
_____

How will I Live this Today?

_____
_____
_____
_____

What does this Reflection mean to Me?

_____
_____
_____
_____
_____
_____
_____
_____

What is your Affirmation to Remind you to Live this Fully Today?

_____
_____
_____

DAY 84

If we will take the time to analyze your life you will see what influences you. What do you read? What do you watch on television? What do you listen to on the radio? Who do you spend time with? Whatever has the majority of your time is your main influence! I know you love the Lord. I know you believe he is God but what do you allow in your space "THE MOST" ? THAT is what is influencing your decision and life process.

What stands out to me in this Reflection?

_____
_____
_____
_____

What do I need to Change to Live this Fully?

_____
_____
_____
_____

How will I Live this Today?

_____
_____
_____
_____

What does this Reflection mean to Me?

_____
_____
_____
_____
_____
_____
_____
_____

What is your Affirmation to Remind you to Live this Fully Today?

_____
_____
_____

WEEKLY REVIEW

THIS WEEK:

NEXT WEEK:

2 **FAVORITE MEMORIES**

2 **WAYS I CAN HELP OTHERS**

3 **PLACES I WANT TO GO**

3 **THINGS I'M GRATEFUL FOR**

1 **THING I WANT TO GET BETTER AT**

1 **HARD LESSON LEARNED**

2 **THINGS I AM LOOKING FORWARD TO**

1 **THING I DID THIS WEEK I'M PROUD OF**

3 **NEW THINGS I WANT TO TRY**

OVERVIEW

FAVORITE
MEMORIES

WAYS I CAN HELP OTHERS

THINGS I'M
GRATEFUL FOR

PLACES I HAVE GONE

THING I GOT BETTER AT

HARD LESSON
LEARNED

THING I DID I'M
PROUD OF

NEW THINGS I TRIED

Made in the USA
Middletown, DE
23 October 2023

41301080R00117